THE FRIED FROG
AND OTHER FUNNY FREAKY FOODIE FEISTY POEMS

Sampurna Chattarji was born on November 17, 1970 in Africa, in a place called Dessie, Ethiopia. She came back to India when she was just eight months old, so she never got to see Africa except in pictures. She grew up in Darjeeling, where she had the most fabulous childhood, walking, hiking, looking at the snowy peaks of the Kanchenjunga and dreaming up stories and poems. She studied English Literature in Lady Shri Ram College, New Delhi, and after graduation became a copywriter in J Walter Thompson, an ad agency, where she worked for seven years. In 1999 she gave up advertising for good and became what she had always wanted to be—a full-time writer.

Her books for adults include *Space Gulliver: Chronicles of an Alien*, which is a poetry collection, and *Land of the Well*, which is a novel. *Ela: The Girl Who Entered the Unknown* is Sampurna's novel for Young Adults, also from Scholastic.

You can find her online at https://sampurnachattarji.wordpress.com/

Published by Scholastic India Pvt. Ltd.
A subsidiary of Scholastic Inc., New York, 10012 (USA).
Publishers since 1920, with international operations in Canada, Australia, New Zealand, the United Kingdom, Mexico, India, Argentina, and Hong Kong.

For information regarding permission, write to:
Scholastic India Pvt. Ltd.
A-27, Ground Floor, Bharti Sigma Centre
Infocity-1, Sector 34, Gurgaon 122001 (India)

First edition: June 2009
Reprinted: September 2009
This edition: October 2015
Reprinted: January 2016, 2019

ISBN-13: 978-81-8477-285-2

Printed at Shivam Offset Press, New Delhi

The Fried Frog

and other funny freaky foodie feisty poems

by

Sampurna Chattarji

Illustrations by Priya Kuriyan

SCHOLASTIC
New York Toronto London Auckland Sydney
Mexico City New Delhi Hong Kong Buenos Aires

For Antara and Tara, with love

Contents

A prelude, a prayer to the Muse

Occult, this thing between words.
Magic me to the next set of sounds.
Travel, song, from heart to beat.
Morph and make believe.

Computer Mice Go On A March

We demand our rights! They squeak.
Call us mice, or else we'll freak!

One mouse plus another adds up to mice,
To call us 'mouses' is just not nice.

Just because we fit in the palm of your hand
Doesn't mean we won't take a stand

For what is and should be justifiably ours—
We'll take our fight to the highest powers!

Just because we [illegible] your toes
Doesn't mean we can't be your deadliest foes.

Unless you give us our grammatical dues—
[illegible]

To cooperate with a right click or a left,
[illegible]

[illegible] page,
And don't ask us to control our rage!

Enough is enough, our moment has come,
Call us 'Mice'—or we'll call you 'Scum'!

Logically graphically comically ME

I'm Sick of Learning Lochinvar

newly dedicated to Ebrahim

I'm sick of learning Lochinvar,
I'm sick of Robert Frost,
Kept stopping by those snowy woods—
Why didn't he go get lost?

And daffodils and babbling brooks,
I don't care if they're pretty,
I'd rather read a wicked poem
About living in my city.

I don't mind the Highwayman
With that hat upon his brow!
But all that happened long ago,
Doesn't anyone write about *now*?

f someone ever asked me
As if someone ever would!)
'd tell them what I'd like
To make a poem good.

'd like a poem about my dog,
Ringgit is his name.
And Ringgit is a currency—
Didn't know that—what a shame!)

Or a poem about my sister's friend
(The two of them are three)
Who comes over to our house
Only when she wants to pee.

Or perhaps a really serious one
About dragons and dragonflies,
A poem with really serious facts
Instead of only *lies*.

No poems about pirates please,
I'd prefer one on sport.
Or a super genius child who
Invented a game of thought.

But who's listening and where can I
Find such poems on the shelf?
Who cares, I know a better way—
I'll write them all myself!

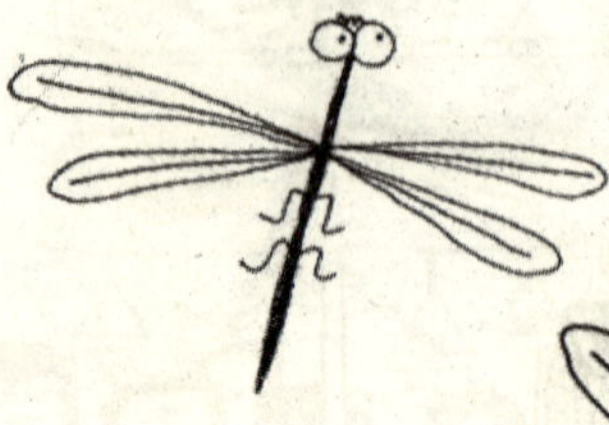

Logically graphically comically ME

I'm pathologically punctual
I'm ecologically bound
I'm biologically beautiful
I'm psychologically sound

I'm photographically ferocious
I'm geographically lost
I'm calligraphically contemptuous
I'm biologically crossed

I'm economically offended
I'm gastronomically glad
I'm taxonomically listed
I'm ergonomically bad

I'm multifariously nefarious
And multitudinously free
So repeat now as loud as you can—
Logically graphically comically ME!

A Nature Poem

When they say 'nature'
Meaning mountains, valleys, forests, seas,
All I feel like saying is—Please!
That's not nature to me
And it shouldn't be to you
Especially if you knew what I do
Which is this—
My 'nature' is *my* nature!
The way I'm shy with strangers
Unafraid of dangers
Friendly with cats
Crazy about hats—
That's my nature
And that's 'nature' to *me*!

Flash

Scrawny city-kitten, railroad-tail,
tiger-crouch in a crevice,
looking for a scrap, a rat, a mouse,
a sore on its fur, its purr like a snarl,
now seen in the sun, now gone.

Fabulous Beast

for Maahir

There's a fabulous beast in my neighbourhood—
It's called the Garbage Truck.
It arrives every morning and gobbles up
Everything that *we* call yuck!

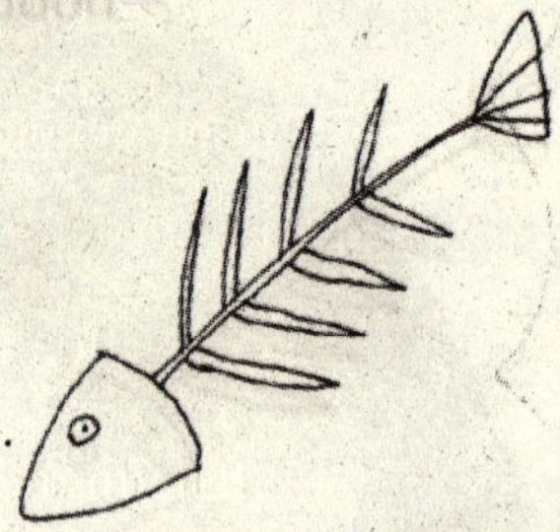

Its mouth is in its rear-end
And it's always gaping wide.
In its head it's got a human
Who takes it for a ride.

When it's done its rounds you'll see
Stuck between its pointy teeth
Curls of peel and plastic bags
Fish bones and shreds of meat.

And when it's full, it spits it out—
Wack-thhoo—onto a garbage dump.
And that's why this monstrous beast
Never gets fat or even plump!

On the Way Back Home

A shadow falls
across my face.
It's about to rain.
I tie my lace.

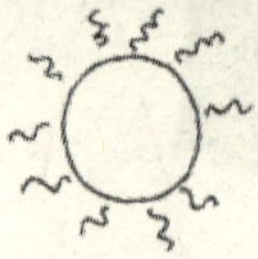

Holiday Poems

for and in collaboration with my then seven-year-old niece Sitara

Walking

My aunt and I walked a long way.
I got tired but my aunt did not.
When I play basketball in school,
I don't feel tired but I feel hot.

An ant

I stepped on an ant today.
My aunt stepped on an ant yesterday.
What if my aunt had been an ant?

My erasers look like food

One looks like an ice cream cone
Another looks like a cake
The third is a strawberry jelly tart
So yum you can't tell it's fake.

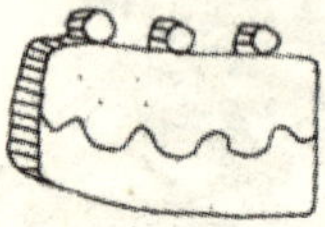

Dry noodle soup

I sat down for dinner.
I thought it was noodle soup.
But it was *not* noodle soup.
It was *dried* noodles.
Or *fried* noodles.
I was even happier than before.
And so I ate oodles!

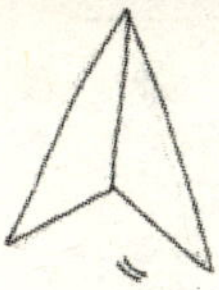

Airplane

I was making an airplane.
My aunt wanted to help me, so I let her.
When I tried to help *her,*
She said: 'No thanks.'
So I said: 'No problem!'
And I read my book.
When I looked up,
The airplane was a mess.
Finally she let *me* do it.
My airplane was perfect.

If only she had left me alone from the start!

Action Heroine

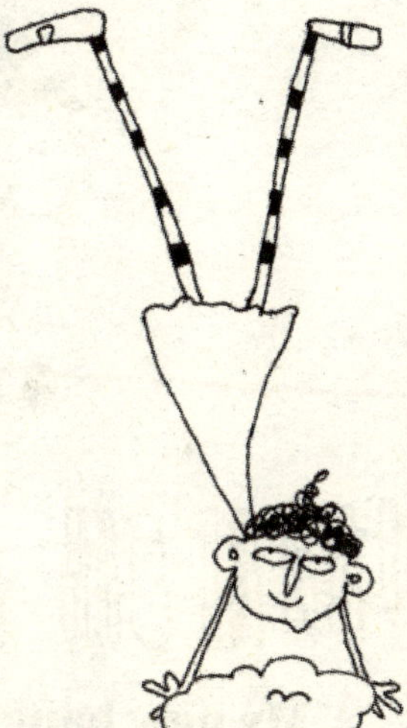

I watched *Hanuman* today
And when I came back
I was running and swinging
And jumping and walking
Just like little Hanuman!

My uncle bought me a flute

We went to a restaurant called 'The Village'.
There was a cow sleeping on the ground.
There was a lady riding a bullock-cart
And then I heard a bang-bang sound.
Three men were playing the tabla
And a stall-keeper was selling some stuff.
That's where my uncle bought me a flute—which I played so lou
My mum wished she had an earmuff.

(But the worst part was—there *were* no earmuffs!)

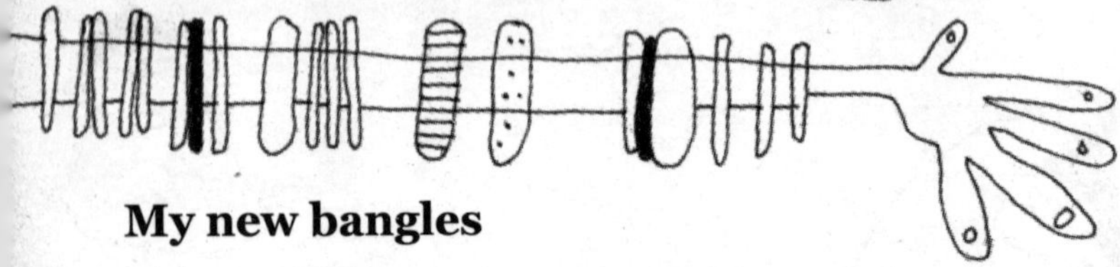

My new bangles

My new bangles are bright gold
And they shine in the light.
My aunt's glasses are quite old
And still they shine in the light!

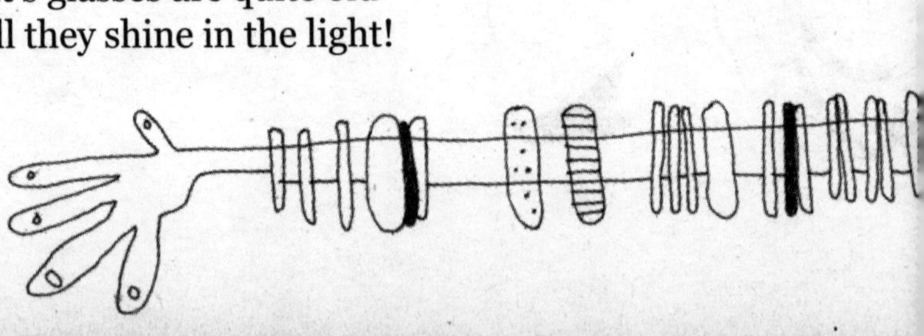

Life

A giant on a plane is plain absurd.
A clown on a comet is pure comedy.

A metro ticket in a city without a metro is impossible.
And that's how life is—absurd, funny, impossible.

Loco

I know many weird adults—they're practically all loco.
Like Aunty Sheila who likes dipping her toast in cocoa.
Or Uncle Shiva who wears seven thick and shiny chains
To tie up all his trunks when he's travelling in trains.
Or my elder sister's friend who calls herself Shampoo
And talks in frothy bubbles, as if her name were true!
Or my father's childhood friend who calls my father 'Candy'
Although my father's hardly sweet, unless he's had a brandy.
Or Uncle Jai who once went swimming in a lovely fishtank,
Then got arrested for breaking rules *and* because he stank.
But the weirdest of the weird adults is the one I love the best
For no other reason but that she always outdoes the rest—
And that's my Aunty Pi who eloped with the neighbour's son,
A wicker basket, a cocker spaniel and a Kalashnikov gun.

Just Wondering

Do tailors have tails?
Do sailors have sails?

Do novelists make lists?
Do chemists make mists?

And if they do—

Are the tails straight or curly?
Are the sails happy or surly?

Are the lists long or short?
Are the mists cool or hot?

Word-Balloon

I'd like to ride a word-balloon,
High up in the sky,
Made of words like *bandicoot*
And *caravanserai*.

Or perhaps a word like
GARGANTUAN (that's big)
Or another one like *excavate*
Which really means to dig.

Sometimes I'll use lighter words
Like *ethereal* and *fey*,
Sometimes I'll use heavier ones
So I won't drift away—

Like *conjugate* and *colossal*
Like *octahedral dome*
Like *ponderous* and *parliament*
Like *tabernacle tome*.

But the brightest ones will be
The best, the shiny happy words
Like *scintillate* and *radiate*
They'll fly like hummingbirds.

Don't ask me where I find them,
They're in the dictionary,
And back home I feed them all
To my pedigreed canary!

Spoooky!

(to be shouted out loud whenever the word appears)

A tall man with a red mouth that smells of blood and sizzling green eyes of fire—

Spoooky!

A woman with a bulgy bag that wriggles under her arm as she climbs up the stairs—

Spoooky!

A bend in the road where the shadow of a tree falls like a skeleton onto the stones—

Spoooky!

A light in the night that goes off then on then off then on then off then on then OUT—

Spoooky!

A noise under the bed that sounds like the shuffle of wet limbs slooooooooowly dragging—

Spoooky!

A house on the hill with rust on its doors and a face in the window that melts into mist—

Spooooky!

A head that turns around to say hello and then doesn't stop turning and turning and turning—

Spooooky!

A person in the mirror who looks like you walks like you talks like you but is NOT you—

Spooooky!

An evil grin without a face—

Spooooky!

A hand on your shoulder—

Spoo

Dropping out of nowhere—

Ooo

A voice in your ear yelling—

Spooooky!

Grand Dad

'You have big ears,' she told her Grand Dad, 'ears like a monkey's.'
'Indeed I do,' he said, and waggled them to make her laugh.

'You have big ears,' she told her Grand Dad, 'ears like the handles of a jug.'
'Indeed I do,' he said, and pretended to pour.

'You have big ears,' she told her Grand Dad, 'ears like hoops I can swing by.'
'Indeed I do,' he said, bending gently over her. 'Want to try?'

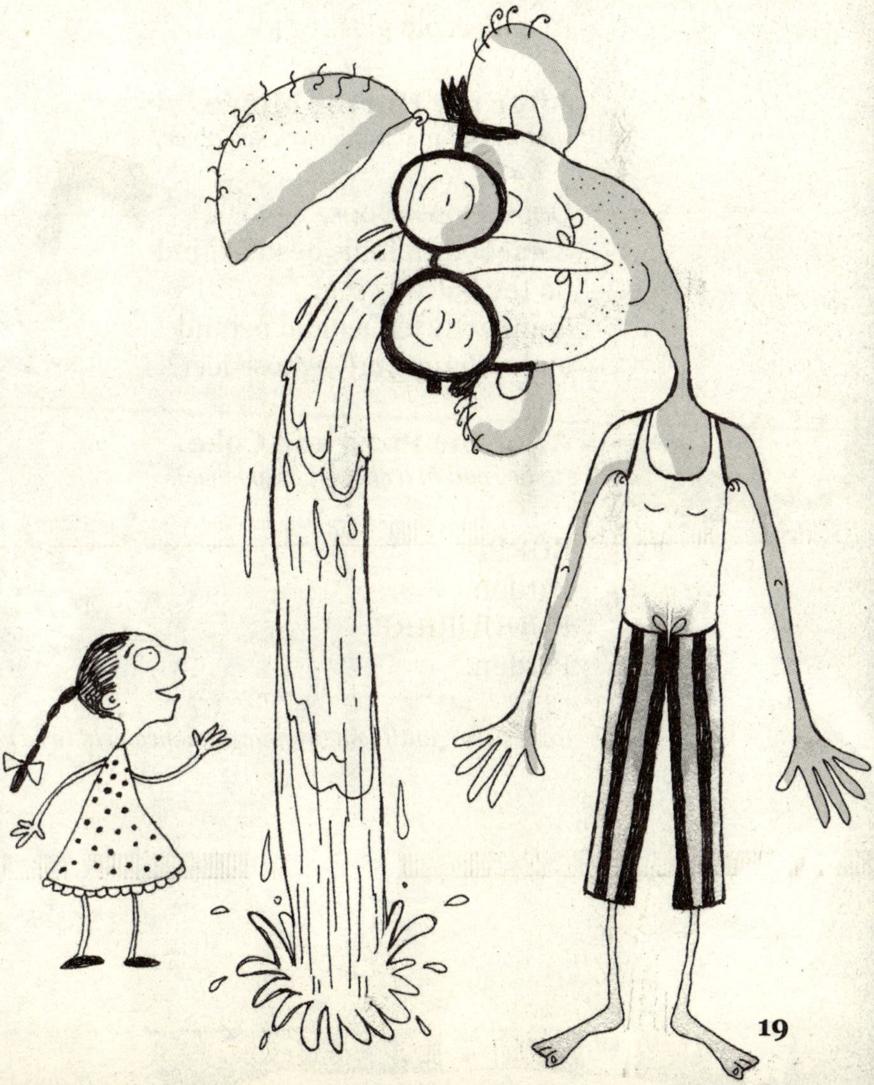

A Series of Aftermaths

(with voice instructions for maximum effect)

After the Journey

(to be read in a super-snobby voice)

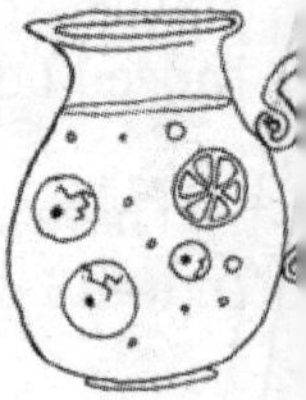

Take your eyes out
And put them on the table there...
My maid will pick them up
And put them
In a *nice*cold glass of ice.

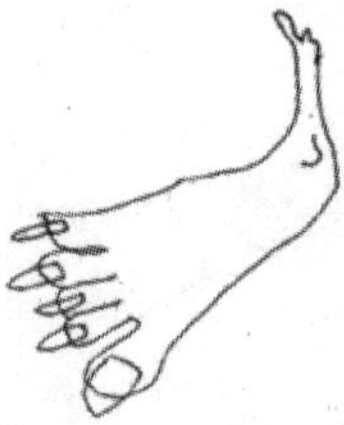

After the Horror Movie

(to be read in a panic-stricken voice)

Oops. Oops. Oops.
Somebody left his head behind
on the balcony seat.
Somebody left a hand behind
and—*oh my god*—whose feet?

After the Pizza and Coke

(to be read in a cheesy, fizzy voice)

BURP!
Pardon.
BUUUURRRP!
Pardon.

(and so on, until you or your audience gets tired)

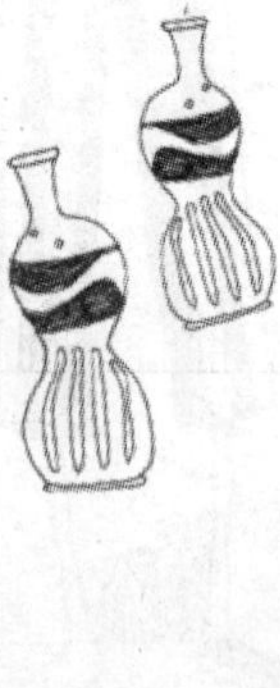

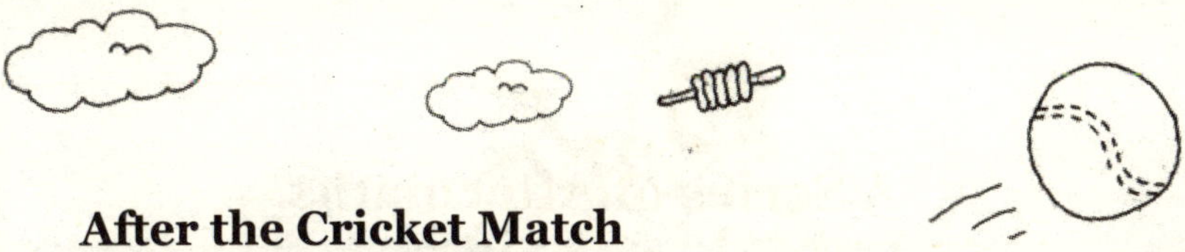

After the Cricket Match

(to be read in a triumphant or defeated voice, depending on which side won)

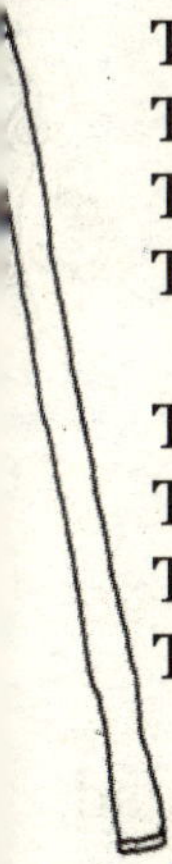

The ball danced to the music and the bat went flying,
The stumps were bleeding and the wickets were lying.
The pitch was black and the crease was rumpled,
The field was plowed and the tickets were crumpled.

The players were drummers, the umpires were hands,
The stadium was radium and the flags were lands.
The faces were clocks and the waves were sea,
The checks were crossed and the crowd was free.

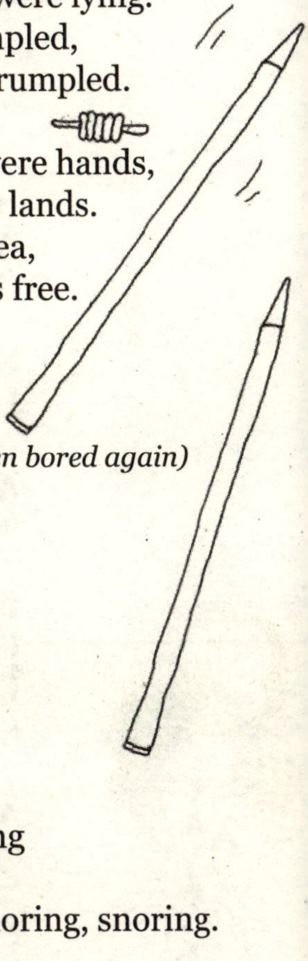

After the Holidays

(to be read in a voice that is bored, then excited, then bored again)

Life is boring, boring, boring
So bring me
A big red herring
The Strait of Bering
A ship's steering
A bear's earring
A deed of daring
A game of glaring
Before I start
Snoring, snoring, snoring.

After the Birthday Party

(to be read in an adult voice)

Now that I'm ten I have all the presents of mind
I will ever need.

After Maths

(to be read in a couldn't-care-less voice)

I'm divided subtracted confused
I'm confounded I'm bemused
I'm multipliable by zero
I'm unviable as a hero

After the Illness

(to be read in a very feeble voice)

I'm peaky and pale.
I'm spotty and stale.
I'm not allowed junk.
I think I will flunk.
I wish I were dead.
Or back in my bed.

Rock Faces

I tried looking for faces in the clouds, but honestly, I failed.
All I saw was cloud and yet more cloud, cirrus and long-tailed.

But once—

When driving through the Western Ghats, I saw faces in the rock.
I saw a bulldog pup and a turtle and a giant foot in a grassy sock.

The Intelligent Young Reader's Complaint About Fiction
for Aabir and Arvind

If only they didn't describe everything all the time!
Like the face of the hero or the scene of the crime,
Or the colour of his eyes and the smell of the rose—
If only they described the stinky-smell of his toes!

If only they didn't make it all so pretty and neat,
All the loose ends tied, the endings happy or sweet,
And the puzzle all fitted and the riddle explained.
If only they didn't think our brains would get sprained

As we imagined, deduced, and filled in the blanks,
Never losing our way as we rode our think-tanks,
Zipping through the plot, and tying up the threads—
If only those novelists examined their heads!

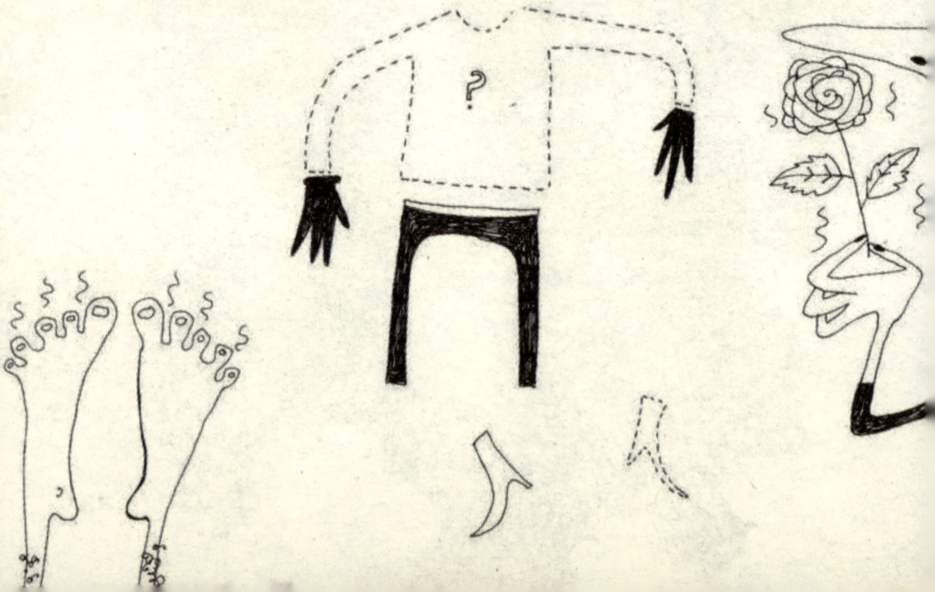

The Dos and Don'ts of Unusual Kids

Unusual kids don't barf in the school bus after a picnic.
Unusual kids do like *Lord of the Rings*, the book more than the movie.

Unusual kids don't whine just because they have homework.
Unusual kids do turn cartwheels in the streets of their childhood.

Unusual kids don't pretend they haven't got any sisters.
Unusual kids do enjoy their own company the most.

Unusual kids don't like Barbie dolls and everything that's pink.
Unusual kids do make me feel like I am one of them.

More different than ever before

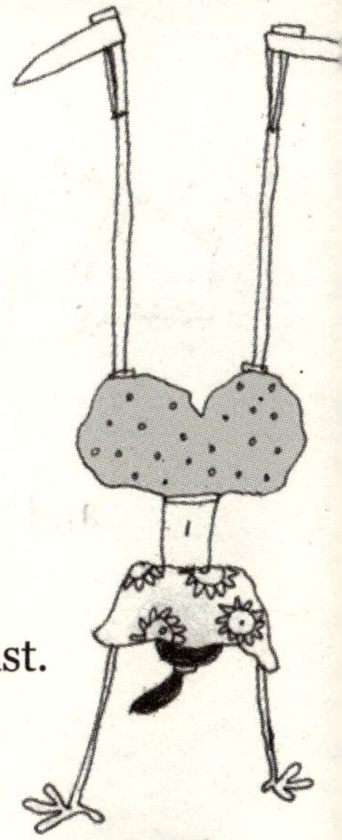

Boys Meant Skinny

i.

Boys meant skinny.

'Xactly the same as us
'xcept we couldn't do handstands
without our bloomers showing
and that stopped being funny pretty fast.

We ate, sang, sat, ran
like one big body
made of many little parts.
Knees tore with equal suddenness,
rivalries flared and died
with equal speed.

On sports days,
at scout camps,
us girls in shorts,
now 'xactly the same as the boys,
'xcept everyone looked at our thighs
as we compared bruises
and insect bites
while waiting busily
for jeeps, for bells, for lunch.

Mud, paint and ink
made our hands blotchy
and our cheeks pink
with praise and exertion.
And one word at a time,
the universe came creeping in
without our knowing,
just part of our blood and bones and games.

ii.

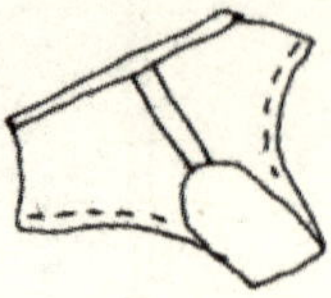

Boys meant funny.

Not parting with their secret
Commando comics,
not looking at our faces
and not speaking any more when spoken to.
Turning from friends
into enemies
faster than the earth
which takes an entire day.

Fleeing as we ghostwalk
down the corridors,
two girls in a tide of shrinking boys.
We're Moses, we tell ourselves,
trying to hide the hurt, *they're the Red Sea*.

The truth is a mystery.
Something must have happened
between yesterday's happy Mowgli dance
and now.
Surely something silly
that we'd fix,
if only we knew how.

iii.

Boys meant stupid.

Look at the way they talk
and the way they walk,
showing off
when we aren't even looking!

Heroes, that's what *they* think they are.
Well, we know better,
and what's more,
we don't need them,
coz we've got *us*!

iv.

Boys meant cute.

Look at him, d'you think he likes me?
Oh I hope so.
Please please please let him like me
Or else
I don't know what.

v.

Boys meant men.

Not one of them like that cute guy
from the boys' school—
the one I never got a chance to talk to—
and not one of them quite safe.

The women know what to do,
laughing and bossing them around
with pretty painted hands.
But I am lost and ill at ease.
Uncertain how to talk, sit, smile, look
at men
without bruising my face with blood.

Until, slowly,
the discomfort goes,
the fear disappears,
the friendly smile walks in,
the comradely hello speaks up,

and suddenly—

vi.

Boys meant friends.

Easy-to-bum-around-with-friends.
Share-sob-stories-and-silly-jokes-with-friends.
Hold-hands-not-fall-in-love-with-friends.
Talk-about-books-you've-read-with-friends.
Dance-till-you're-a-dizzy-spinhead-friends.
Good-to-go-home-late-with-friends.
Sometimes-better-than-girlfriend-friends.
'Xactly-the-same-as-me-friends—

Only more different than ever before.

My First Death

The chapel
down the slope
overlooked the garden
and the grave.

There,
I sang hymns
to a person
I was told was God.

I enjoyed the singing,
the little grey books
I had just learnt
to read,
each word the first word,
all new again.

I enjoyed chasing the syllables
of the ululating
Glo-o-o-o-o-o-o-ria!
A game I played, me against my
deepest longest breath.

I barely noticed the cross.

And then,
one rainy morning
on the chapel steps,
I sat and mourned
with the full force of
my seven years
my very first death—
the Padre who sent sweets
flying magic through the air
into our waiting hands.

Pansies waved at my feet
as I wept,
not knowing why,
just that class was called off
and yet no one was happy,
that a person
much older than me
had gone somewhere
he must not
have wanted to go.

It was an adult act,
that mourning,
and I was already growing
past that moment
into all those future funerals,
not one of which would feel
as real
as the one
I didn't understand.

Like the cross I didn't see,
and the chapel
and the hymn.

High-Altitude Sickness

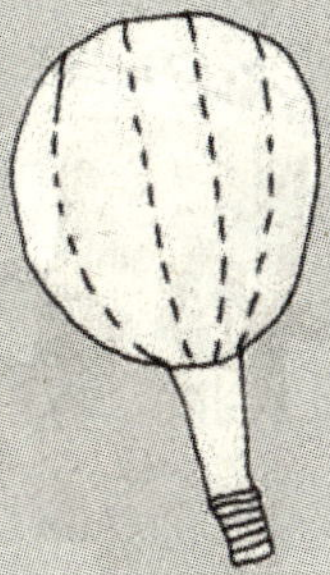

The higher the curve
the lighter the head
the whiter the clouds
we spoke out loud.

The colder the air
the quicker the huddle
into woollies
forgotten all winter.

All winter spent in the plains.
Three cold months turned
hot smoky seething
itching to be back.

The thicker the fog
the slower the crawl
the lower the growl
of the engine.

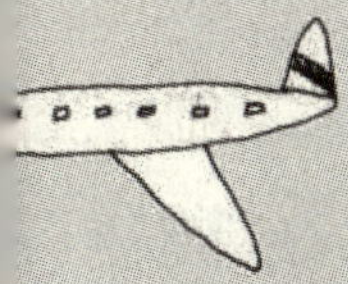

The faster the dark
the gladder the light
cutting windows
out of the night.

So it always was—
my mum, plains-born,
sick on her way up,
me, on my way down.

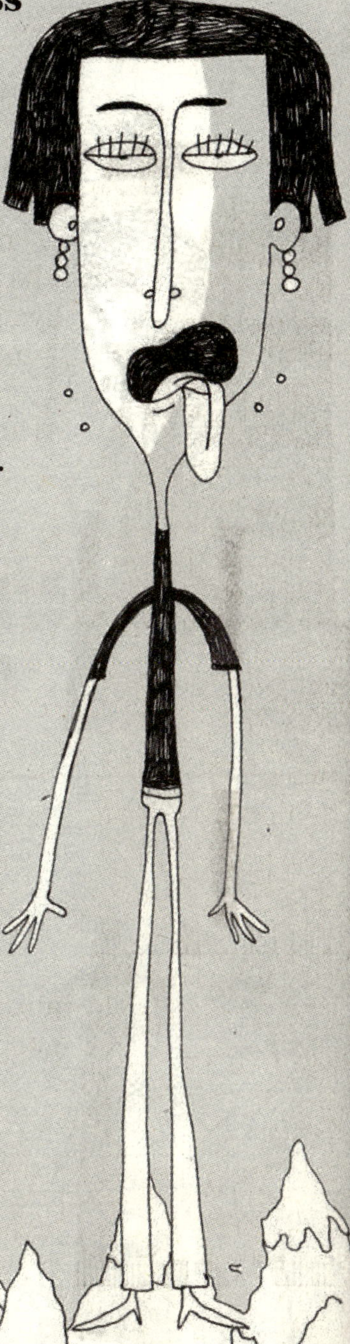

Used To Be

Used to be
just waking was reason
to go mad with joy.
Fed, dressed, kissed,
then sent hurtling
past the lawn
past the field
past the slopes
past the trees
past the breeze
past the town
past the high Himalayan peaks
into this—

A desk
in a room
in a city.

Used to be
just the thought
of a book
unread
was cause
to lose my way
through a day.
Rapt, not hearing a word,
just waiting for class
to be over
and then

walk run race home
open the door
fling down the bag
drink up the milk

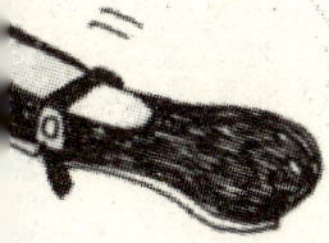

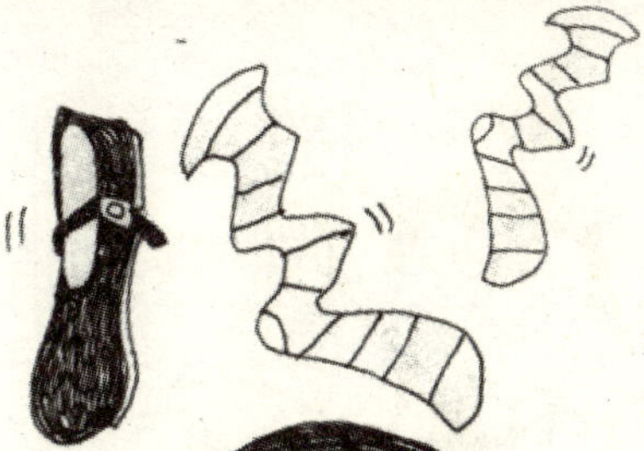

throw off the shoes
jump on the bed
take out the book
and sink into—

A quiet depression.

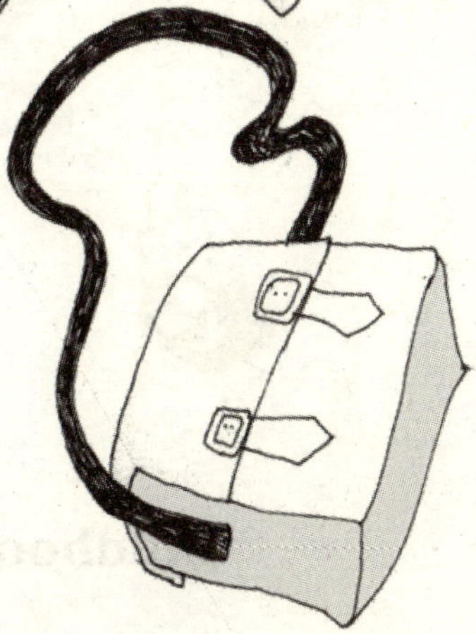

Used to be
just the sight
of yellow light
in mist was poetry,
hot bread and jam,
a hiding place
in a wall
behind a fern
where a single
orange marble winked,
firestruck and swollen,
a candlepowered tin
floating titanic in a tub.

Proud
of the red apple cheeks
I stole
from my little Bhutia friends,
proud
of the Kanchenjunga
I fitted into my window,
proud
of the giant night shadows
I spread across the wall,
I sit—

Too close,
too distant
from where I began.

Childhood, Crossing the Highway

An hourglass made of cane
under his arm, he crosses
the highway.
On his head,
wrapped in a
familiar red cloth, goes that
other taste of childhood—*bhel*!

Girl, Adopted

Her heart beats hard against your chest.
She is four, all bone and longing.

Already she has a past.
She remembers everything,
except that she was abandoned.
She has parents, grandparents, uncles, aunts, cousins.
Dark brows meet when she frowns.
She loves your fingers running down her spine.
Her eyes are singing: 'You are mine.'

But how easily you could have lost her.

She could have turned American, then,
or Norwegian (fjords floating
in her eyes). She could have stayed
unchosen, anger collecting like dirt
under her fingernails. She could have run away,
twice-orphaned, begging at gleaming cars.
She could have drifted, nursing hidden scars.

All bone and longing, she is four.
Your heart beats hard against her chest.

My Opia

A tale of lost love and lenses

i.

One eye is blind,
my lens fell out.
One eye can see,
but what good
is that to me?
Where should I look
for that curved
piece of glass?
By the side of the road,
in the khud off the grass?
Will it be ground
into mica,
that polished piece of sight,
sharing the spark
and glitter
of breaking broken light?
Has it fallen
into the path
of a car
climbing up the hill
with an awful squeal?
Or—and this is what I dread—
will it crunch right *now*
under a blind,
naughty-boy heel?

ii.

Minnie Four Eyes he called me.
'Huh?'
'Haven't you seen *Love Story*?'
'No.'
'Oh.'

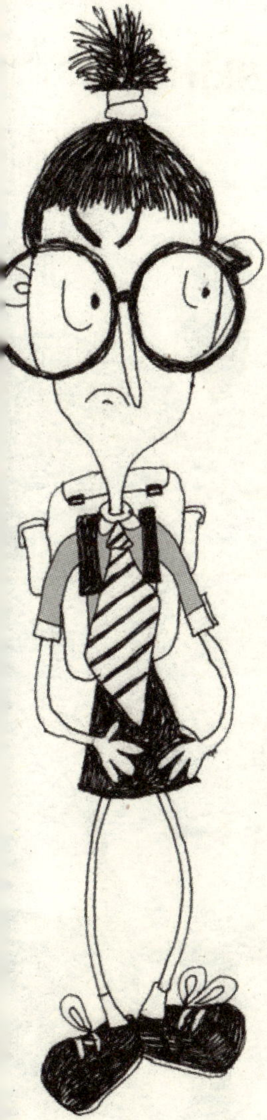

The conversation paled.
He was walking me to school,
across the field, down the slope,
tall and mistycool.

My lenses were lost.
My glasses were back,
perched on my nose,
so ugly, so morose,
so plainly in the open
for the world
to see and say—

'There goes the bookworm
with the shadows
in her eyes.
There goes Minnie
Feeble Four Eyes.
She reads on the mountain
under the quilt,
right into the dawn.
She blinds herself
by yellow moonlight
until the batteries
are gone.'

On Blushes, Jealousy and Skirts

i.

You're making me blush.
You're not *saying* anything,
But it's making me blush.
Don't say anything,
I kind of like the hush,
Just you and me,
You, making me blush.
In any case,
There's no *need* to rush,
I could sit here all day,
With you and my blush.
It feels hot on my cheeks
And I have to say
That my heart feels like mush,
As if you had kissed me
Instead of simply—
Making me blush.

ii.

I'm jealous of your hair.
I've said it, so there.
I'm jealous of the way
It looks like hair spray
Has made it set and shine
The opposite of mine
Which tangles up in knots
To complement my spots.
I'm jealous of your skin,
So smooth and flattering,
Not a single ugly boil
Ever shows up to spoil
Whatever plans you make,
It's more than I can take,
It's more than I can bear,
I'm jealous of your hair.

iii.

Skirts.
I like mine short.
Shorter.
Shortest.
Hot.
Hotter.
Hottest.

But when it's time to put one on
I suddenly feel shy.
Long.
Longer.
Longest.

I wonder why.

Variations on the Word – 'Play'

Play me a tune I can whistle easily.
I never was very musical.
The only thing I played was pranks.

Playtime always got over too quickly.
I always played the fool.
And you? You played with fire.

All work and no play makes Jack a dull boy.
That's what they told us,
without quite believing it.

Play on, my friend. One day, we will need a place to return.

The man in the yellow sou'wester

Here We Go Round the Mulberry Bush

In the shade of a London park,
mulberry juice ran red
from my palm
right down to my elbow.

I carried the stain until evening,
the colour on my lip explainable,
the colour on my arm concealed.

Plucking mulberries in a park,
how strange it felt, how sweet.
Remember that song we used to sing—
Here we go round the mulberry bush?

Well, this was no bush!
To me it looked as large as a tree—
a brooding tree, a hive of purple bloom,
a place where morning seemed like noon.

Blue Heron

for Marileta

I never guessed I could get blue leaving this place.
This lake with its American-Indian name,
Chau-tau-qua, soft rhythms I can sing.

The boat is emptier now.
Earlier—packed with laughter,
the sun falling on faces suddenly dear,
the breeze snatching voices away,
throwing caution and hair to the winds—
the lake had seemed so much smaller.

Now, it is the boat that seems smaller.
Now, the sun is setting,
the air is a chill on my arms,
and in my heart this sorrow.
We could be out at sea.

I cling to my seat, and just as
I find a way to breathe
that rises and falls with the waves,
so that we seem, lake and I,
like one linked and fluid thing,
we're docking—
the clock-tower sudden
before us, a presence of light and stone.
A bird floats silently by,
wings ghosting into me.
'Blue heron,' says the man at the wheel.
'Shy bird. Lucky, I'm told, to see it.'

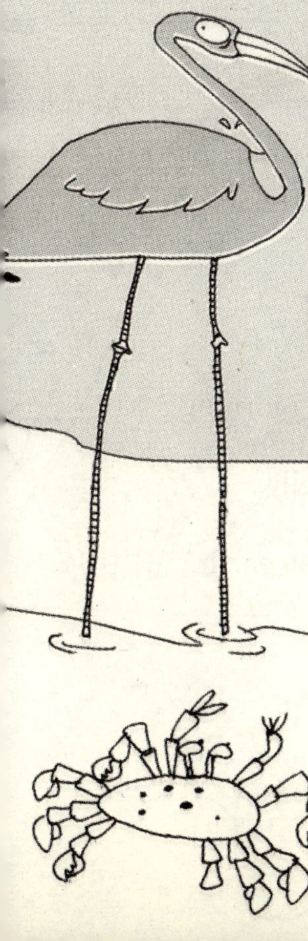

One of three lucky girls,
walking back to a room that is home
for one more night—
is that me wordlessly praying,
giving thanks to the bird, the boat, the shore,
singing thanks to the blue, blue moon?

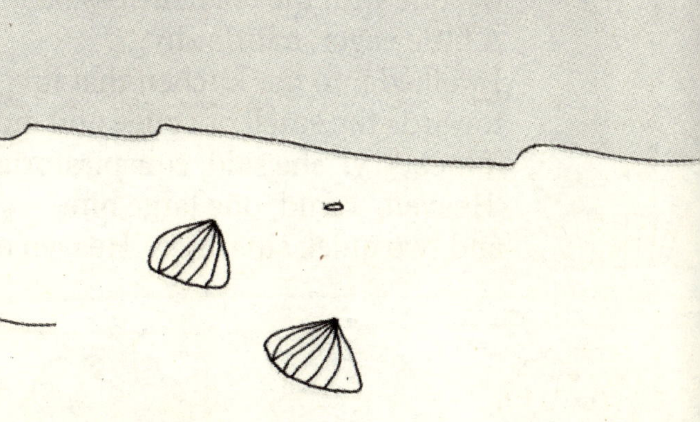

Yogurt and Cinnamon Dessert with Rose Geraniums and Peach

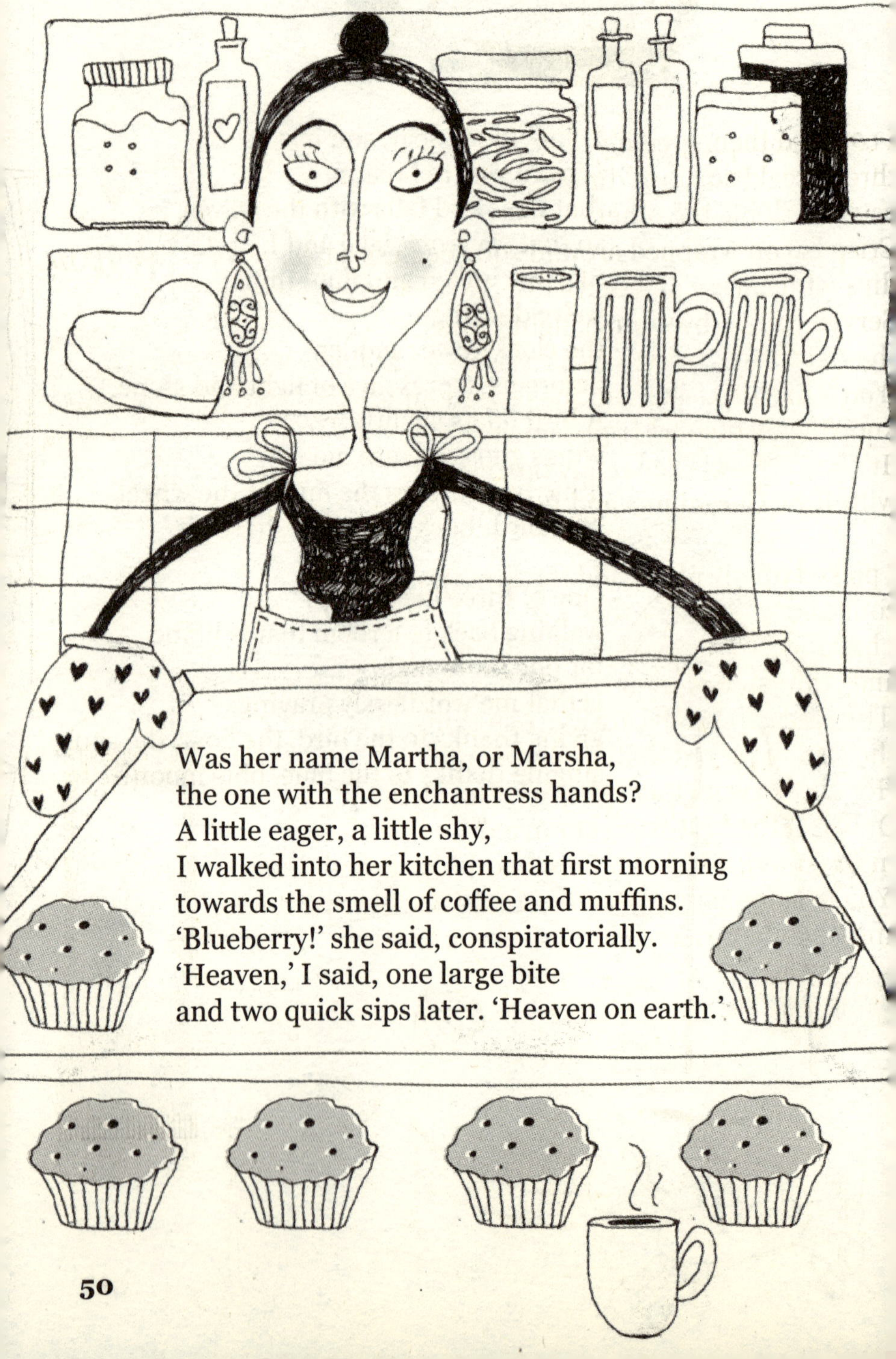

Was her name Martha, or Marsha,
the one with the enchantress hands?
A little eager, a little shy,
I walked into her kitchen that first morning
towards the smell of coffee and muffins.
'Blueberry!' she said, conspiratorially.
'Heaven,' I said, one large bite
and two quick sips later. 'Heaven on earth.'

I counted them greedily,
hree breakfasts, two dinners,
each outdoing the other.
Crisp bacon wrapped around soft seedless dates,
dips with cheese and herbs.
Served course-by-course, light pastas,
the right wine, voices reverential as we ate.
You'll like this,' she said the last evening,
knowing by then where I came from.
It's Yogurt and Cinnamon Dessert
with Rose Geraniums and Peach.'

picked up my plate, and the first spoonful
conjured up a taste I thought
had forgotten, curd steamed with sugar
and cinnamon, a treat my mother made.
The rose geraniums are an Irish thing,'
she said, 'I picked that up in Ireland.'
Her cheeks were flushed. Was it my delight?
Or was it the heat from her oven?
ndia America Ireland. Cinnamon yogurt and peach.
You're astonishing, Martha,' I said, for Martha it was,
and I was happy and close, so close, to tears.

Stopping by a Fishing Village on a Summer Afternoon

With due apologies to Robert Frost

A day hot enough for ices!
Like children,
we lick our scoops
and stare out at the boats.

The sunshine glow
of the man in the yellow sou'wester
holding a fish in his fist.
Fish and chips, crackly in a box.

No one wants to climb back on the bus.
And so, cranberry ice cream with apple
postpones the moment of departure,
melting hotly on our tongues.

Da Iawn*
for Mererid

If you haven't heard these words before,
You don't know what you've missed.
For these are the words you want to use
When you have just been kissed.

Or when you've won the hockey match
And brought home the silver trophy,
Or made it to the Scrabble team
By spelling 'catastrophe'!

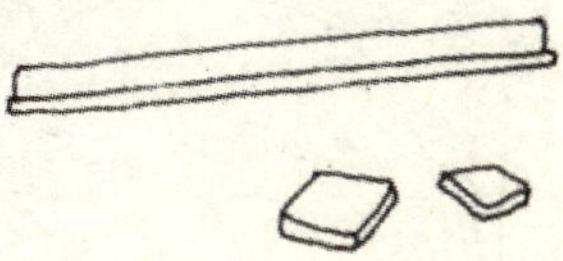

You use them in celebration,
You use them when you're glad.
You use them in congratulation
But never ever when you're sad.

They are a gift from far away,
Each word ringing like a chime,
My friend from Wales taught them to me
And now I use them all the time!

*(*pronounced 'Daah-Yaowwn')*

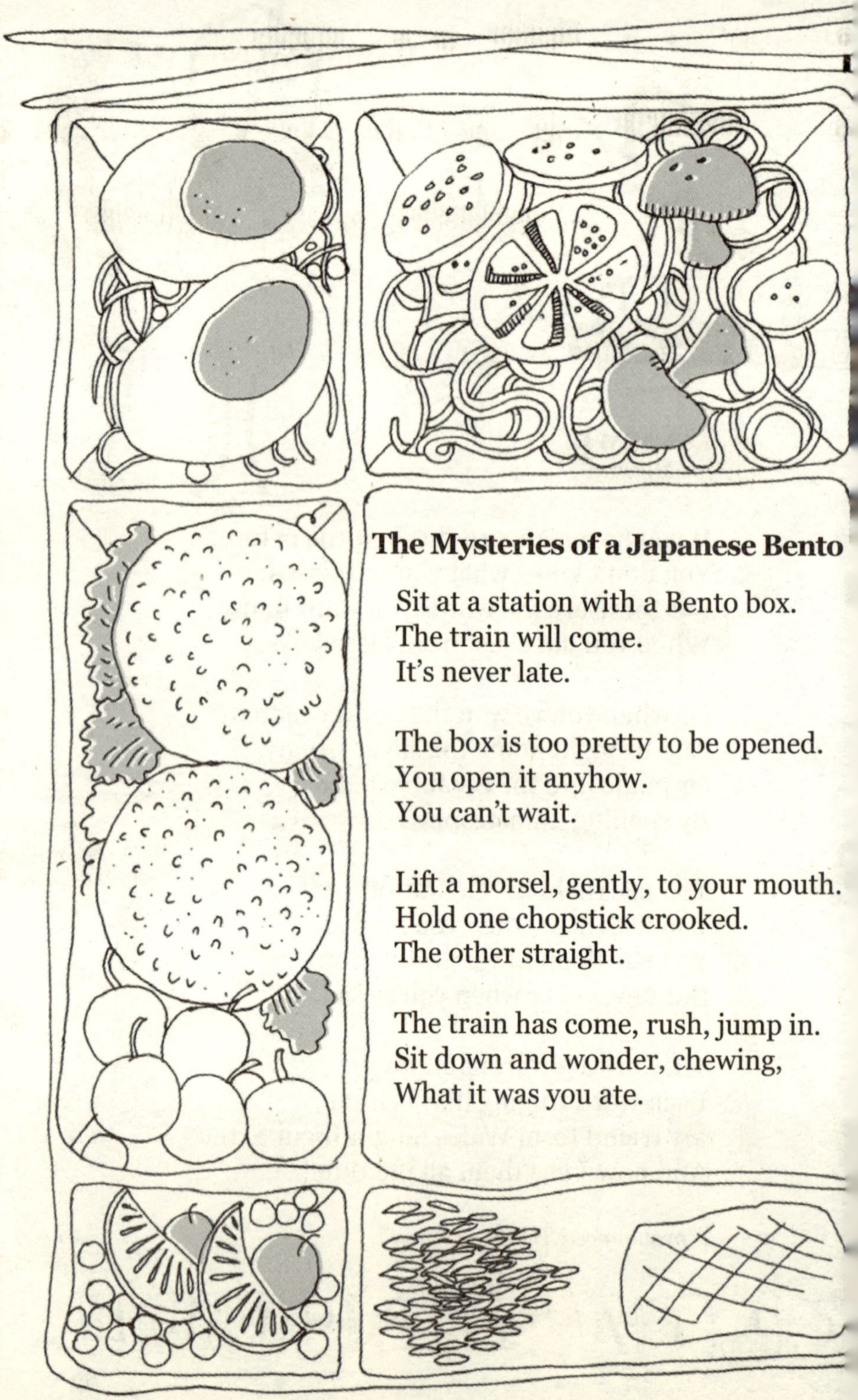

The Mysteries of a Japanese Bento

Sit at a station with a Bento box.
The train will come.
It's never late.

The box is too pretty to be opened.
You open it anyhow.
You can't wait.

Lift a morsel, gently, to your mouth.
Hold one chopstick crooked.
The other straight.

The train has come, rush, jump in.
Sit down and wonder, chewing,
What it was you ate.

Ginza A.M./P.M.

In the morning Ginza whizzes with cars.
In the evening it sits down with babies
and old men (red umbrellas, white chairs)
and watches the sun go down.

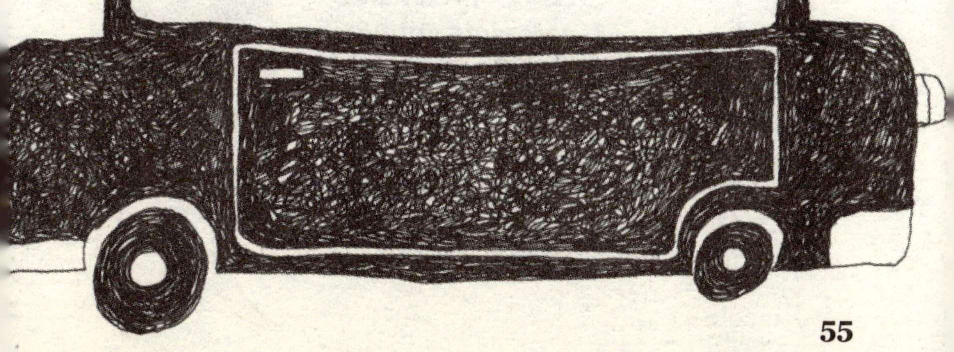

Entries
on a journey through South India

Every river
tempts her

shed skin
jump in

swallow the evening sun.

Girl talk

Can you
keep a secret
lagoon?

Thallasery

That pose is perfect

Long-oared hands
caressing stillness

Knees turn to water

White-heron flutter
in my eye

Observation

Safety is a net
of signs everyone can read
at ninety kilometres per hour
avoiding collisions
with the precision of bats.

Honavar

Cat crossing road. X marks the spot. Cat, crossing river.

Narial at Kumta

newly dedicated to Neha Vaz

Calabash,
sweet
with the salt of the sea.

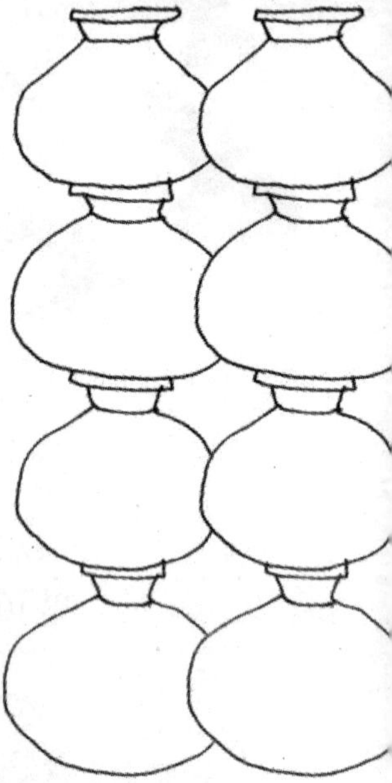

Kasargod

Yellow dress
on brown door
Shadow-child
flirting with sun

Cement ship off National Highway 47

Beached whale
stranded
on a sea
of weeds.
Hull prow
porthole
just so
many
shipwrecked
words.

Clockwork, the earth turns

Epiphany

for Nayana

Every Tuesday, the frogs fly off the pages of the book I meant for your parents.
And yet, you are the one who loves it most, the epiphany of frogs as they fly.
Do you dream of them, larger than clouds or lily-pads, lighter than feathers?
With their eyes on the back of their heads, do they say hello, goodbye?

Elevators and Escalators

Elevators and Escalators are cousins.
Elevators like listening to music.
Escalators don't.

Elevators are moody, they break down.
Sometimes the old ones—the ones
with the grille doors—get stuck between floors.
In movies, it's always the Elevator
that comes crashing down a zillion storeys,
ending in explosions of electricity and toasted hair.

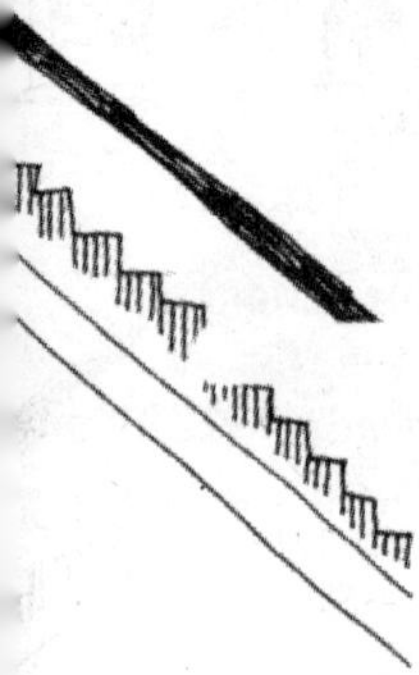

And Escalators?

Escalators purr smoothly up and down,
secretly sticking out their tongues at their cranky,
noisy, disaster-prone, twice-removed cousins.

Elevators have men to run them.
The men sit on stools in uniforms
and press the buttons smartly
every time someone goes up or down.

Escalators are lonely.
No one runs them. They run on their own,
up and down, endlessly.
Escalators hate Elevators
when it comes to the question of men.

Escalators know that there are two kinds
of humans on this planet.
The ones who are cowards
and the ones who are brave.

The brave ones *always* take the Escalator.

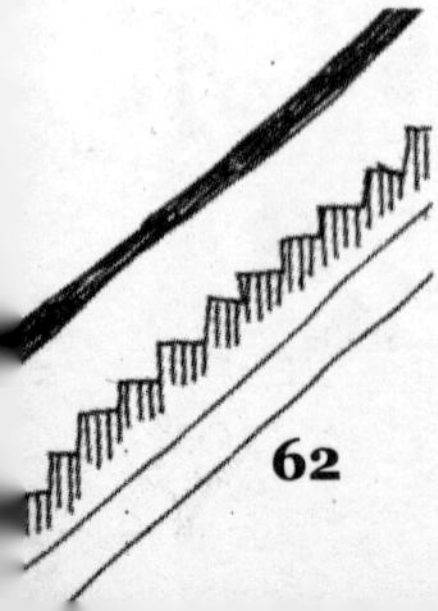

The scaredy-cats take the Elevator, not daring
to put their feet on the running treads,
they *dread* the fact that Escalators *never* stop,
except at night, when the malls are closed,
and even then they run, endlessly,
in the nightmares of the Elevator-people.

Escalators sneer at the Elevator-people.

Escalators are smooth and sly
and love those who love to glide,
love pointy painted toes,
love hems of shiny silk,
love soft and brushing hands.

Elevators are private. They hate crowds.
Takes only 16, you moron! they want to say
to the 17th person who squeezes in
at the very last moment.

The Elevator's dearest wish is to be empty all day,
with no one but a little boy for company,
tall enough on tiptoe to reach the highest button,
small enough to know that riding up and down
is their shared idea of heaven.

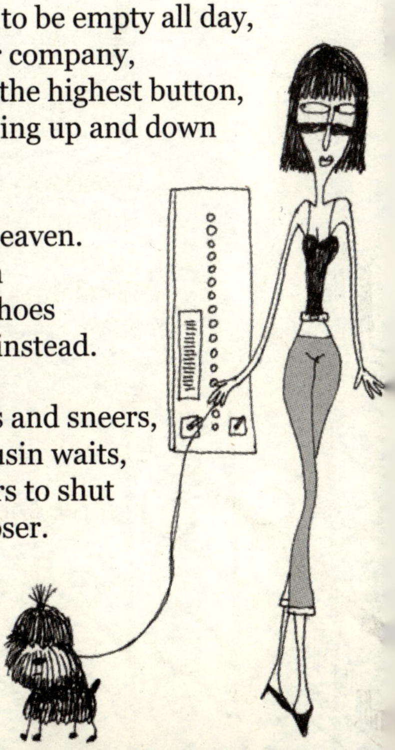

The Escalator has no idea of heaven.
Its only wish is that short men
would stop wearing elevator shoes
and switch to escalator shoes instead.

Until that day arrives, it glides and sneers,
it runs and hates, while its cousin waits,
patiently, silently, for the doors to shut
and the sky to come a little closer.

Lonely

She must have been lonely,
the old woman with the broken voice
who sat on her balcony every evening
shouting 'Larissa, Larissa' every two minutes.

Larissa never answered, from wherever she was.

I wish she had, just once.

Unseen

Sunken Garden, 5 p.m.

There is talk here, and laughter.
Thick white cups of thick sweet tea.
Chair-legs dig holes into just-watered grass.
The light changes.

No disturbances except a passing 'Hello!'
from a friendly familiar or two.
This sunken patch of land unseen
behind the car park.

High up on the 21st floor, unseen
but for one pair of eyes,
three workers hang in bright orange jackets,
tiny against the great white scaffolding of sky.

Such precision in their movements.
Clockwork, the earth turns.

Twenty-o-nine

On the twentieth of September
at nine past eight
in the year two thousand and nine
this is what the digital clocks said:
20:09 20-09-2009

And we said:
Ah, the poetry of numbers!

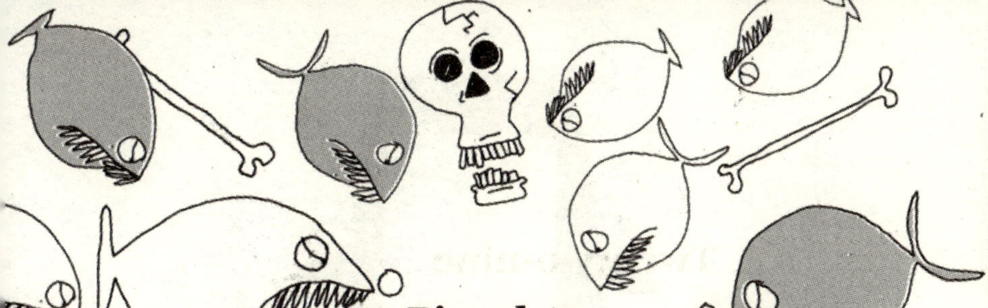

Piranhas

Picked
to the quick
Stripped
of everything
Barecoldandshivering
Dissected
subtracted
from the sum of all its parts
Bones sticking out
making neither head nor tail
sharpetched
against the light
A hieroglyph
of slant and curve
of straight
and slightly bent
Twisted remnant
of the feast
a fish rippedtorn
by delicate fingers
those piranhas
daily demolishers of flesh
stained
until licked
and
polished
clean

'Go Away'

Or what the intolerant said

The ground beneath my feet
is shrinking.
If you come any closer
I will scream.
If I smell your animal breath
upon my cheek,
I will scream.
If your words don't echo mine,
I will scream.
If your faith doesn't bow to mine,
I will scream.
If your thoughts don't follow mine,
I will scream.
I have planted my feet here
and here I will stay.
So cut out your tongue.
Go away.

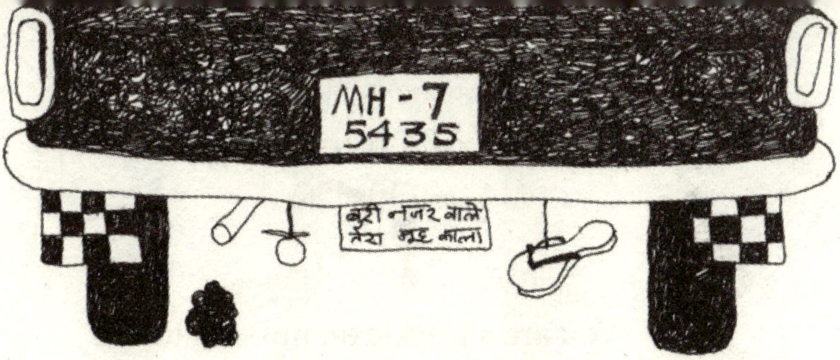

Taxi

newly dedicated to Harleen, Nissim, Nittal and Sanjana

You streak speed,
black and yellow creature of the tar,
you sweat metal.
Your stillness is a mirage,
vanishing in the heat-haze flicker
of a summoning hand.
You singe skin.

Your insides betray you,
velvet foliage twisting with fingers,
the roof a mirror,
the dash an altar to three gods
and one hanging CD, rainbow-tinting the air.

The music of horn and brake is yours.
Your vagaries define you,
spit-hawk strategies of dodge
and dare, the surly trudge,
the start and stop through smoke
and sludge, finger-snatching the fare.

You ferry souls,
black and yellow trawler of the city,
you spark conversations.
Your safety is a bomb,
bursting in the split-second terror
of a left-behind bag.
You survive everything.

In memory of the bomb blast at the Gateway of India, on August 25, 2003. The bomb was hidden in a taxi.

A Kind of Love Song

You are a prickle on my skin today.
A leaf on my tongue.

You are a pair of swinging legs
from the edge of a table today.

You are a desire to run.

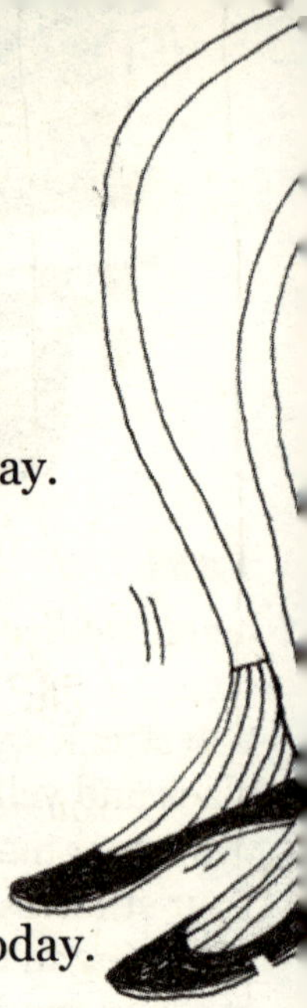

You are an unstoppable giggle today.
A kite unattached to a string.

You are a pair of eyes chasing eyes
in the playfield today.

You are a little blue thing.

You are a secret chamber in my heart today.
An open-window-word.

You are a pair of hands
holding the light for me today.

You are a whisper overheard.

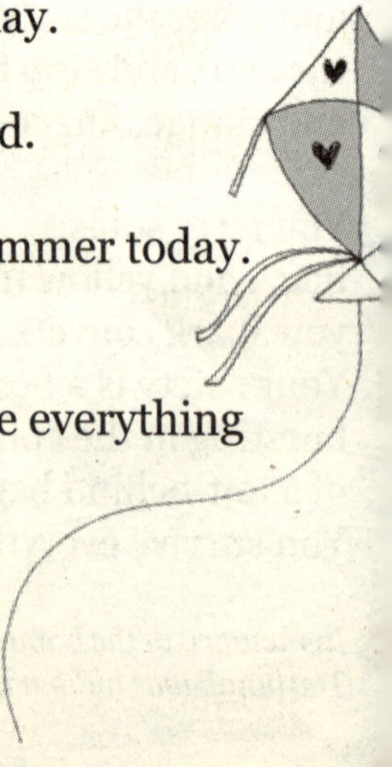

You are a strangeness of summer today.
A sudden tingling of rain.

Warm as my breath, you are everything
but yourself today.

How long will you remain?

Meditation on a Painted Egg

You may have a heart of gold, but so does a hard-boiled egg.
- Anonymous

Perfect ovoid of apple-green marble,
I cannot tell what bird is painted on your shell.
No forked fang no birth pang, just the fine brush
of furling feather full-formed.
Not the golden egg of fairy tale,
not dawn, not fragile, not eaten, not born.
I see conspiracies in your shape.
I see enclosure, and escape.

By what process does Babel turn into a bagel?

Via babble and bauble, bubble and burble, burgle and bugle?

Or, by the simpler expediency
of
dropping
a Bee?

Oh, how the misty are fallen!

A town on tour at the top of a tower takes a tumble.

Alpha gamma beta bets played against the odds of bodkins.

Language is a glorious game.

And clarity begins at home.

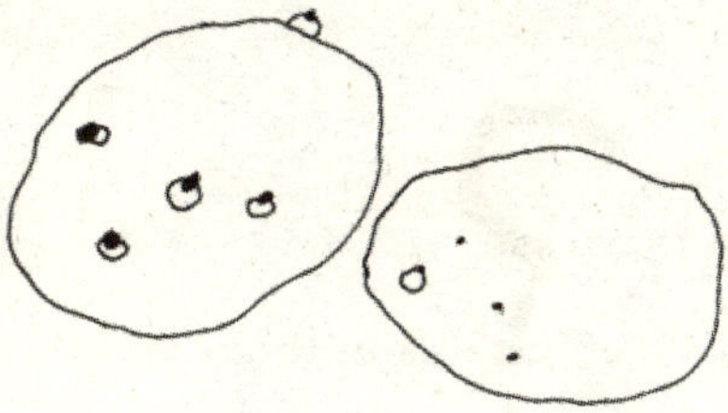

Try Describing

Afternoon

A sack of potatoes
bulging with the weight
of a thousand closed eyes
and skins.

Hunger

The hollow place
where the echoes
of your taste buds go.

Telephone Call

Shrill and sudden
sting of a silent
black-coiled snake.

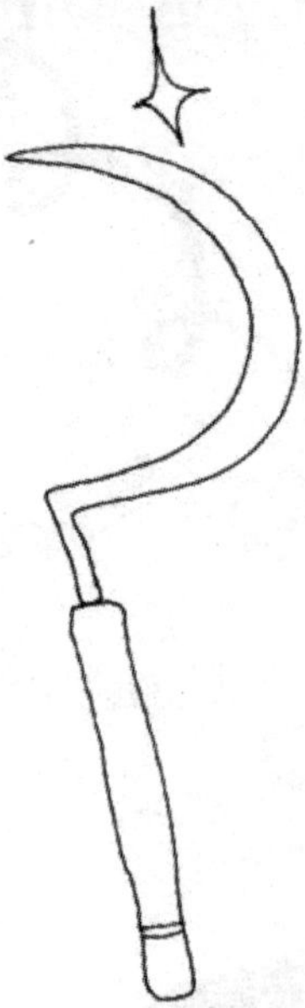

Why

Doubt-shaped
like the sickle
of a question mark
full-stopped
by a drop.

Bed

Four-footed animal
carrying my belly on its back
flopped and ready to sleep.

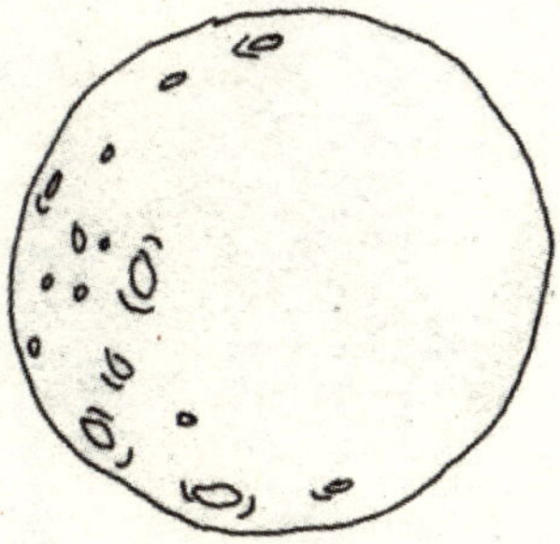

Alligator shoes ride elevators to the moon

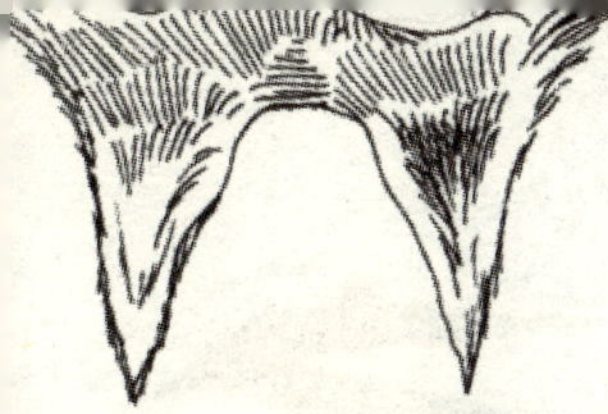

fear and denial are two orange cats
held together by a golden rope.
their eyes are blue.
and you?

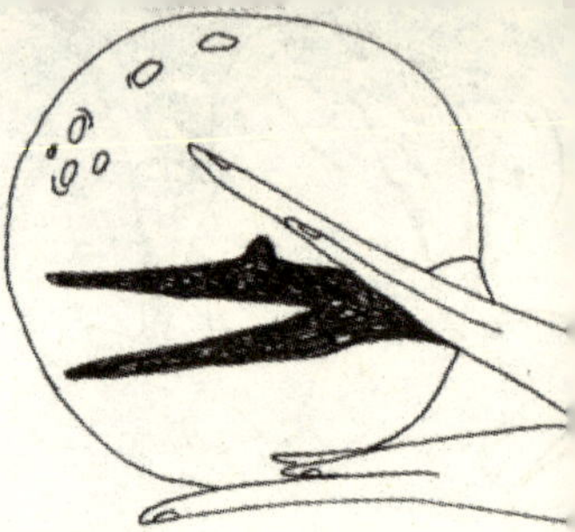

See You Later, Alligator

(After a While, Crocodile)

The shadow puppetry of hands
Crocodile mouths on walls
Made-up faces
Of glass

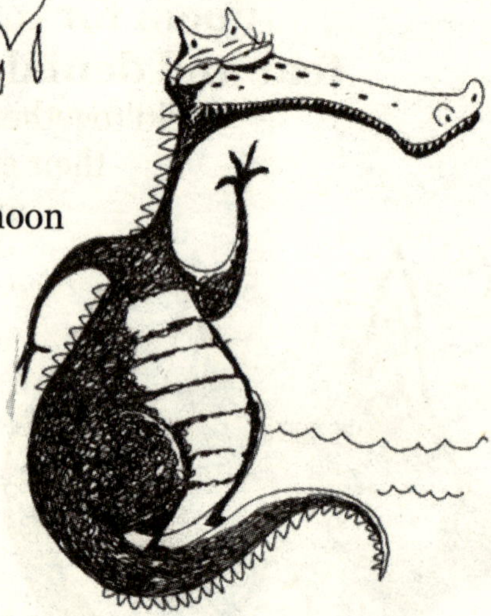

Alligator shoes ride elevators to the moon
Swallow the pins-and-needles sky

Foolish croc and greedy wife
Waiting for the monkey heart
To arrive
On a platter
On a current of water
In vain

First they eat the air then the hair of the nearest tourist

Fibreglass birds in a dying swoon
My alibi is sky
Clean hands leave prints everywhere
Somebody was framed
That much is clear

The weather is killing
Smokeswirl windhowl
After a while
We all leave

Even the crocodiles fail to hold us with their wicked teeth

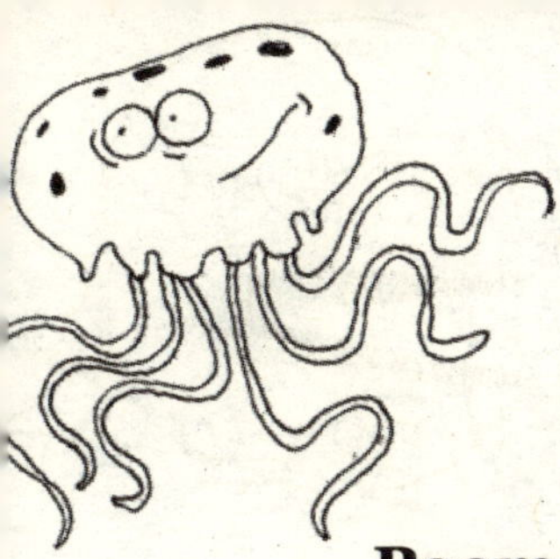

Poem for my Tortoise

We called him tortoise because he taught us
- Lewis Carroll

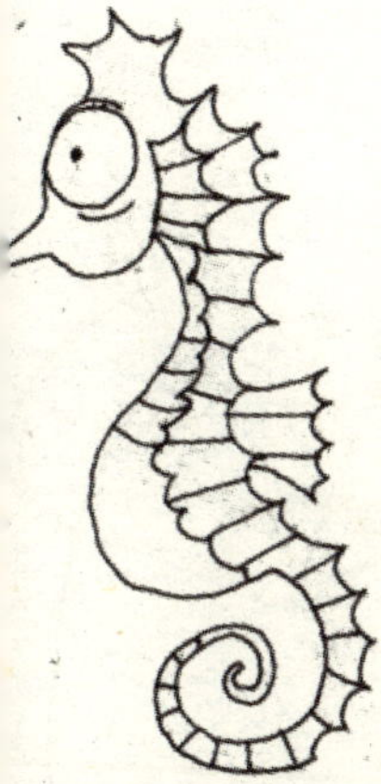

Sea horses race you to the shore.
Jellyfish coax you to eat more.
Mermaids mother you,
smother you with flowers.
Anemones teach Japanese
to help you pass the hours.

You're a water baby,
imaginary maybe.
I know that isn't true
for I have seen you,
blue light of the deep,
swimming in my sleep.

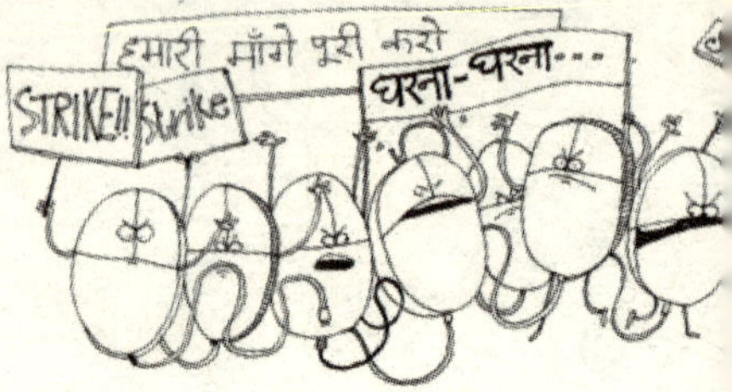

Computer Mice Go On A March

We demand our rights! they squeak.
Call us mice or else we'll freak.

One mouse plus another adds up to 'mice',
To call us 'mouses' is just not nice.

Just because we're in the palm of your hand
Doesn't mean we won't take a stand

For what is and should be justifiably ours—
We'll take our fight to the highest powers!

Just because we don't nibble your toes
Doesn't mean we can't be your deadliest foes.

Unless you give us our grammatical dues—
Dharna! Strike! We downright refuse

To cooperate with a right-click or a left.
Try working without us, your oh-so-deft

Navigators of each scroll-down page,
And *don't* ask us to control our rage!

Enough is enough, our moment has come,
Call us 'Mice'—or we'll call you 'Scum'!

The Crab and the Crane: a retelling

for Ameya, who loves narrative poems

The crab, a chronic idler, was crabby as only a crab can be.
The crane, who lifted crates all day, was longing to be free.
The crab was worried that he'd end up curried on a plate.
The crane was tired of city life and of its gloomy fate.
The crab lived in a murky pool near the warehouse site.
The crane spoke to it at length one smoggy lonely night.
'I'm fed up of this life, my friend,' he said with a rusty sigh.
'I need a place where I can sleep under a starry sky.'
'Blast the stars!' the crab exploded. 'Bother, blast and beaten!
I just need to find a spot where I will not get eaten.
There is a place across the streets they call the blasted sea.
If only I could get there, it would be nirvana for me.'
'I would take you there myself if I could drive, my friend,
But since I can't, this bitter life is our fate until the end.'
'Drive?' the crab said, perking up at last. 'I can drive, dimwit!
I know how to handle gears and wheels, there's nothing to it!
Just lead me to the driver's seat and I will lead us out!'
The crane swallowed, straightened and slowly turned about.

'Climb on, my friend,' he said and that's what the crab did,
Clambered into the driver's cabin and then he blew his lid—
'What sort of dump is this?' he yelled. 'A prehistoric model!
How can I race us to the sea when all you do is toddle?'
'I'm sorry, friend,' the crane said, 'I have no head for heights.
When the human makes me work I get the shakes and frights.
Besides, this is not a good time. Morning is approaching.
Any minute now you may be arrested for encroaching ...'
'Hopeless!' sputtered the angry crab, and jabbed at the switches.
'Why must such a simple thing be so blasted full of glitches!'
In his rage his claws got caught and refused to come unstuck.
And that is when he knew he had gone from bad to rotten luck.
'Save me!' he yelled, but all too late, for the driver was getting in.
'What's this, a crab?' said the driver, and spiked him with a pin.
The crane wept, for now his only friend, crabby though he was,
Was trampled down into the dirt and would never see the shores.

The Electric Caterpillar

An extract from

The Boy Who Had Never Seen A Town: A nonsense-novel in verse and prose

Crowded with bodies
Clouded with noise
Hissing and spitting
Teeming with poise.

The shakier it seemed
The speedier it was,
The more you got worried
The less there was cause.

An electric caterpillar
A racing centipede
A partitioned rattlesnake
A many-windowed-steed.

Wires above and tracks below,
And people in-between,
Looked like this creature
Had haste in every gene.

Taking people here and there
Never getting tired
Back and forth and in and out
So awfully inspired.

A dash of thought
A local dash
A dashing school
All cool and brash

Into it we jumped, us three,
Me and Boy and Croc
And Doggy all entangled
Unsteady as a rock.

Inside the creature snug we sat
Swaying with the motion
While all about us drifted
The most impossible commotion.

Talking fighting eating sleeping
Dreaming cursing reading weeping
Playing cards and singing songs
Buying rights and selling wrongs.

And though on dry land we raced
Many a tidal wave we braced
As surges of people rose and fell
And came and went as in a spell.

And then at last we had arrived
And I could smell the sea,
After all those salty people
It was refreshing as could be.

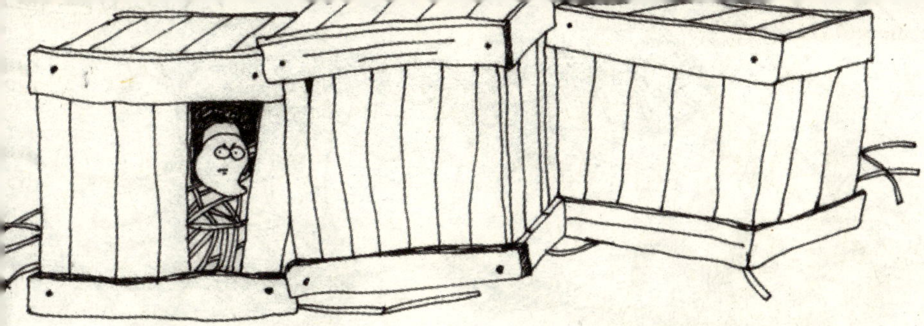

The Mutant Mango

for AR, in lieu of mutant daffodils!

I

Look, juice is not my thing.
Juice sucks, if you'll pardon the pun.
Dribbles down your chin,
stains your shirt, spoils your fun.

No, juice is not gentlemanly.
So here's what I propose—see?
The mutant mango with no juice,
no seed, no skin. Ah! Pure sanity!

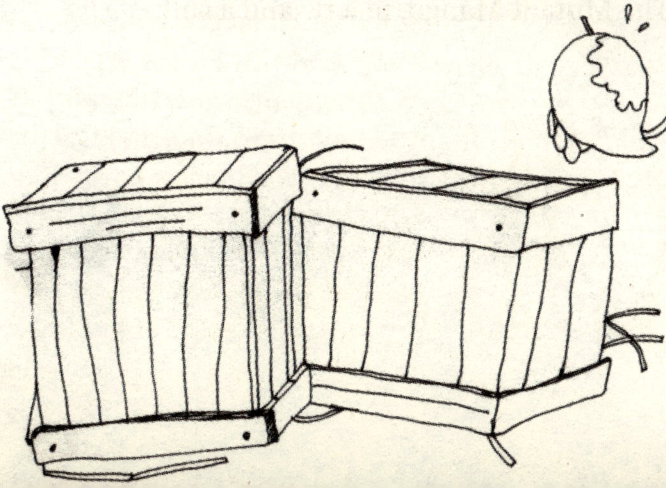

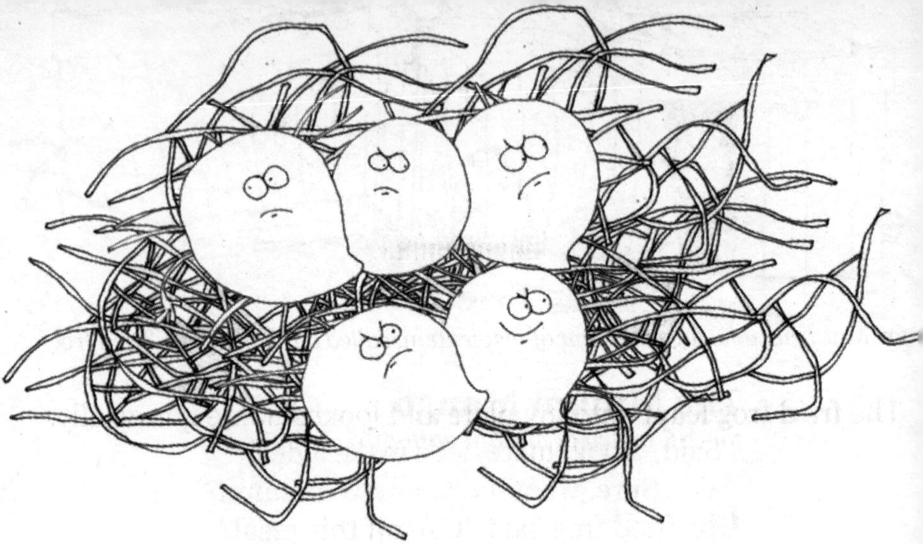

II

Barraged by photons in a crateful of straw
Garaged by truckers in a roomful of raw
Suspended in matter rotated in space
Injected with measures of mouth and of face
Randomly tasted by men in white coats
Structured for travel by planes and by boats
Filled to the brim with colloidal thick juice
Crafted to swim when its skin comes loose
Grafted to colours both alien and fine
Polished by lasers to a pearly-pink shine
Here it is at last—that flamboyant fruit—
The Mutant Mango, in a tie and a suit.

The Fried Frog

for Matthew, who, in a moment of inspiration, called a palak-puri a 'fried frog'

The fried frog leapt onto my plate and looked at me quizzically.
Said, 'Look, mate, let's make a deal.'
I said, 'Sure, what did you have in mind?'
The fried frog said, 'Call off this meal.'
I said, 'You mean, go hungry?'
The fried frog said, 'Yes. Just once. Won't do you any harm,
have you looked in a mirror lately?'
I said, offended by the rude green thing's reference
to my girth (which, I confess, is stately):
'Listen you, you fried greaseball. No one tells *me* how to run my life.'
And with one quick flick,
I popped the fried frog into my mouth, and ate him.

The Fermented White Rabbit

for Meg, who liked idlis (but may not after reading this poem!)

Falling down a hole one morning,
I found myself clutching an extraordinarily soft,
plump, fermented white rabbit
in my right hand and a jar of mango pickle in my left.

'Say when,' the fermented rabbit said, in a sour tone.
'When what?' I said. My grammar is atrocious before breakfast.
'When you want me to stop,' the fermented rabbit said.
'Stop what?' I said.
'Stop you from falling, dodo,' the fermented rabbit said.

That was the last straw.
I dunked the fermented white rabbit in the jar
and watched his brains pickle.
I can tell you that brought back my appetite.
I hummed as I anticipated another delicious breakfast.

The Food Finagle

A capricious culinary caper

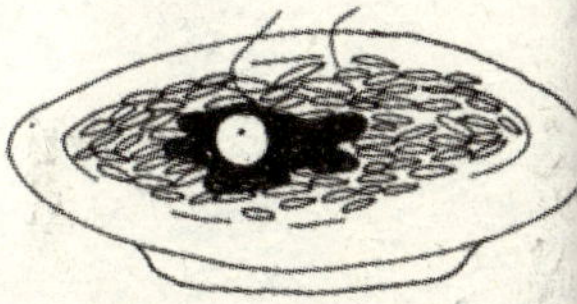

Dhoka!

'He betrayed me, brother, oh how he let me down!'
'So grind him into fine paste, cut him into cubes,
Drop him into burning oil and fry him golden-brown.
Ladle him into gravy that's bubbling full of spice,
And once he's finely simmered, once he's fully soaked,
Serve and eat him up with a steaming plate of rice.'

Upma

Get up ma, it's getting late
I've got to go to school!
Get upma for lunch, they said
Or be a stupid fool.

Luchi*

I like luchi
very muchi.

(**rhymes with smoochie*)

The Giant Puri

Have you seen the giant puri?
It's called the bhatura.
It eats spicey chholey
From a silver katura.

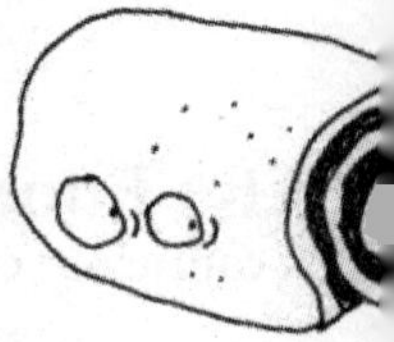

Snakes

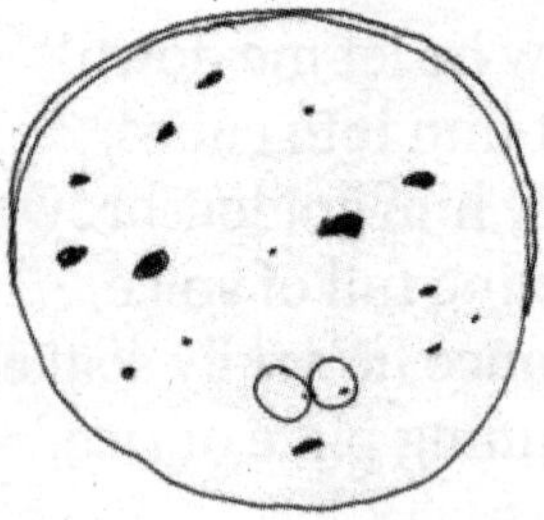

Thepla is a hoopla
Bhaakar is a feast
Dhokla is delicious
And khaakar not the least.

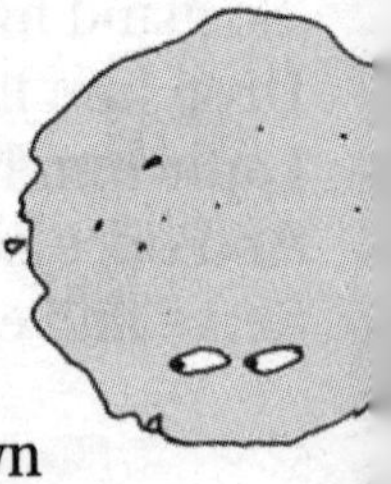

Idli-Pom

Idli lost its fiddli
Dosa lost its crown
Wada lost its wiolin
And let the whole band down.

Very Fishy

There was a fish who called himself
THANKYOUBHERYMAACH.
Till the fishermen caught and salted him
And ate him with boiled starch.

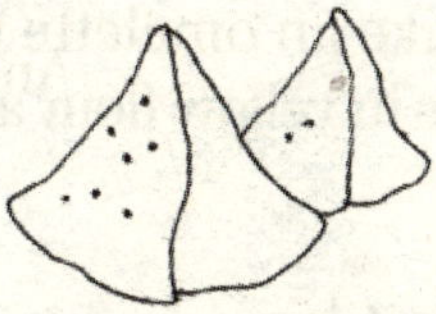

The Samosa Feud

There is an old feud that is waiting to be settled—
Call a 'samosa' a 'shingara' and the Punjabi gets nettled.
Call a 'shingara' a 'samosa' and the Bengali gets mad.
While the two are fighting, there's a plateful to be had.

Explained

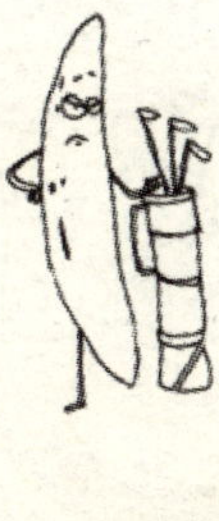

Idiyappam keeps yapping
While Puttu plays golf
Utthapam's my girlfriend
Mutthu's real name is Rolf.

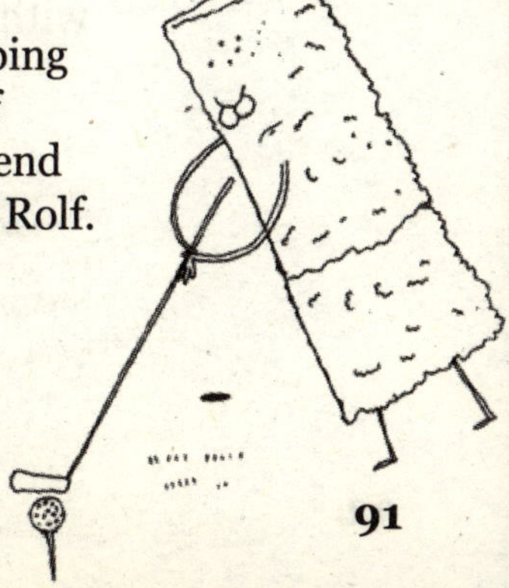

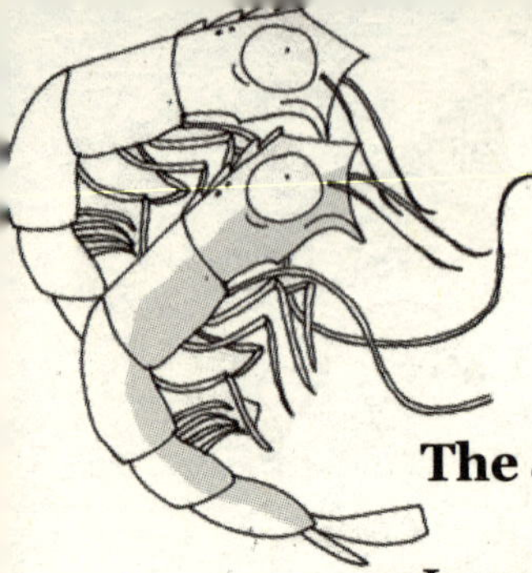

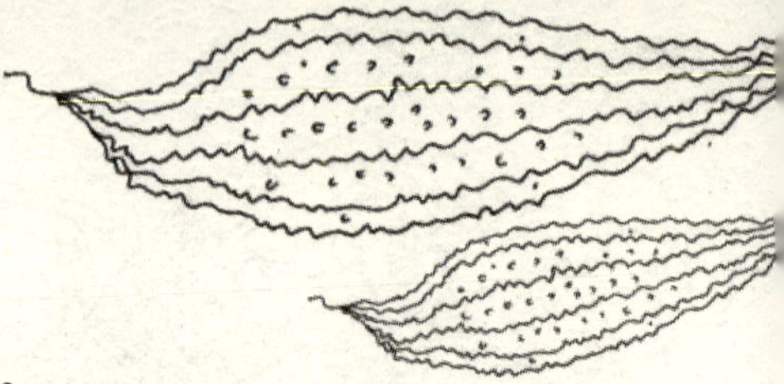

The Jhinga Thinga

In one state it's a vegetable,
In another it's a fish,
Be sure you know where you are—
Or you'll eat what you don't wish.

Easy
A riddle

Q: How can you make an omelette without breaking any eggs?
A: Easy, fry tomatoes in yellow flour and eat it standing on your legs!

Frankie

i.
I love Frankie you love Frankie
Obviously there's some hanky-panky.

ii.
Frankie's not a little boy
who lives down the lane.
He's a fat and juicy roll
with a kabab for a brain!

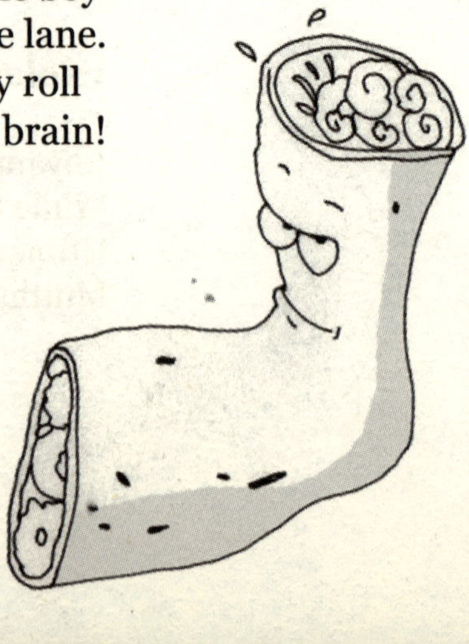

The Battle of Pani Puri

The Battle of Pani Puri isn't over yet.
The West swears theirs is the real thing,
As the North breaks into a sweat—
Their gol guppas are being put to the test
By sweet-toothed people from the East
Who think phuchkas are the best!

Ode to a Luchi*
with apologies for its reappearance

A luchi is smoochie
A luchi is poochie
A luchi is darlinger
Than the sweetest bag from Gucci.

(**rhymes with smoochie*)

The Halwa Hooha

You can make it out of carrots
and serve it for high tea.
Or you can take a fishing boat
and catch it on high sea.

Litany

Grows-on-your-tongue
Fried cream
Filled-with-water
Happy gleam.
Balls of syrup
Sweet curd
Rose fruit
You never heard.
Clove girl
King's feast
Pudding flower
Grows in the east.
Sweet sausage
Eat again
Lady Kenny
Don't say when.

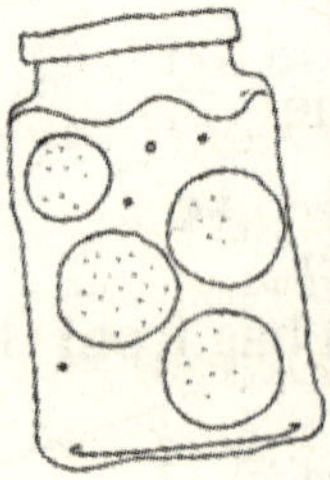

A play on the literal translation of all the curious names that Bengali sweets have

Cuppa *Chai*

A poem for two voices

I like my tea warm and brewed in a pot.
Nonsense, I like mine to be boiling hot.
The flavour of the leaves should be fragrant.
You mean spicy, you mean flagrant!
The colour of the brew so gold and light.
Nah, strong, milky-brown and bright!
Tastes best without milk, my kind of tea.
I'm sorry, but it tastes much worse to me.
Do you take sugar, then? One spoon for you?
Oh don't be stingy now, come on, put two!

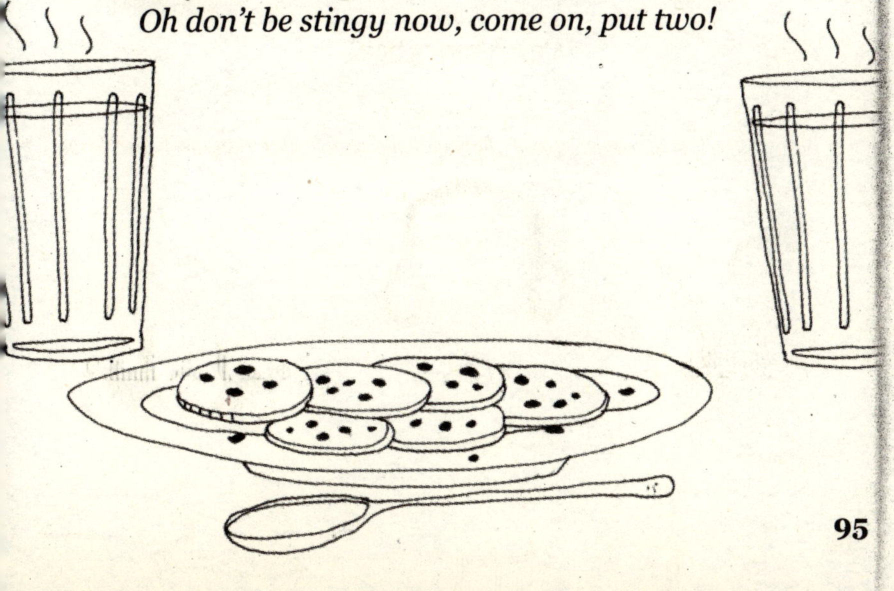

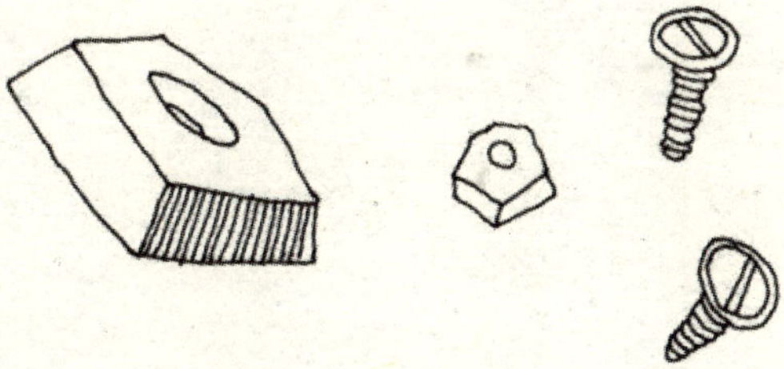

Poetry

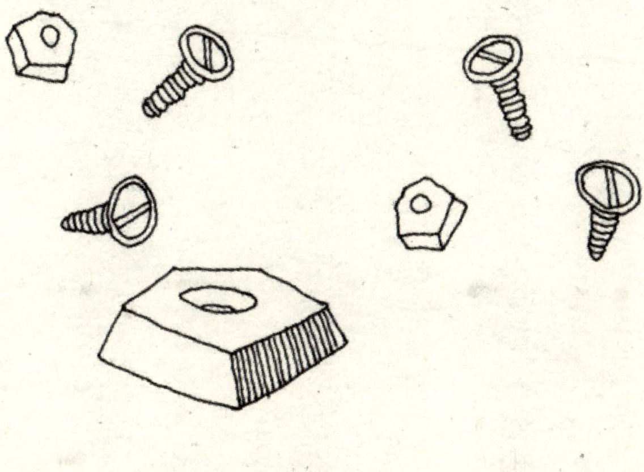

Poetry is for Poets

Poetry is [illegible]
[illegible]
would you really write a poem
[illegible]

Poetry is [illegible]
[illegible]
[illegible]
[illegible]

However
[illegible]
[illegible]
Their poems are read
[illegible]

[illegible]
[illegible]
[illegible] what they [illegible]

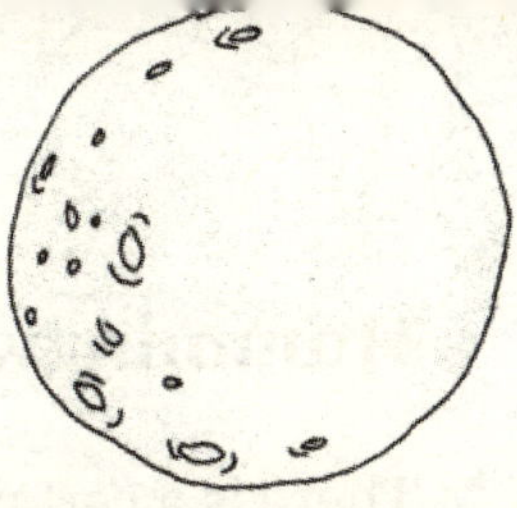

Poetry is for Poets

Poetry is for poets
And poets are all weird.
Would you really write a poem
If you could grow a beard?

Poetry is for sissies
And a sissy isn't me!
I'm a cool-dude hero kind,
The coolest I can be.

Poetry is for crackpots
And why are crackpots cracked?
Their poems are so awful—
That they have gotten whacked.

Poetry is for losers
Who haven't got a clue.
So why is this a poem?
It's what I love to do!

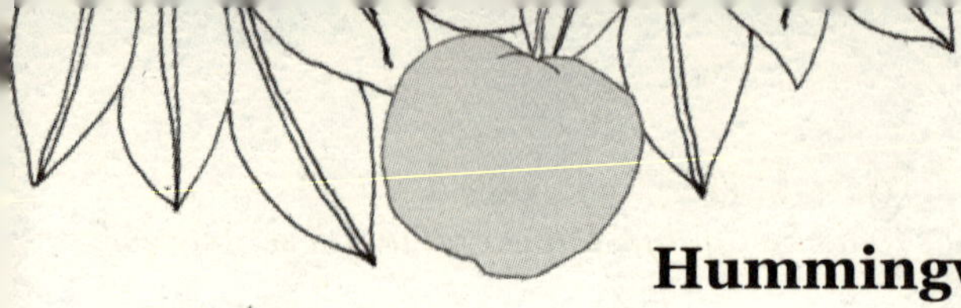

Hummingword

There is a certain kind
of listening
that brings it closer
to my straining heart,
pulse ruby in my throat.
Patient,
tuning to that invisible pitch,
one octave higher
than silence.

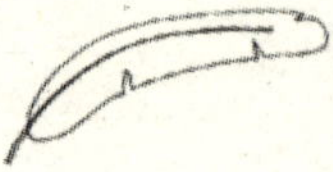

Blood rush of cochlea
and tympanum,
hush.

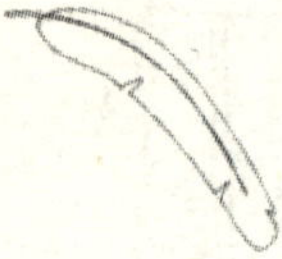

It will come,
with a flapping of wings
a whirring of little beaks
a stirring of tongues.

Twelve-sixty-times per minute
it will beat in my uncurled fist,
my quickening skin.

And in that moment
of perpetual motion,
it will turn visible
at last.

Small, perfect,
a flying jewel,

my hummingword,
longing for nectar, thirsting
to burst into song.

After Archibald MacLeish's 'Ars Poetica'

for Aashya, who said, 'A poem should be funny, simple and in full sentences.'

A poem should be funny
as a clown falling down,

simple
as the meaning of a teardrop.

A poem should be made
of full sentences that reveal

half-hidden things,
full of light and shade,

as full
as your heart when you're happy.

A poem should be funny
as a conjuror's hat,

simple
as that gift of laughter.

Fulfilled by each word
moving towards each thought

like a dancer
into her partner's arms.

A poem should be full of charms.
Funny as a serious man

trying to tell a joke, simple
as Simon.

A poem should be full
of new sounds, empty of noise,

a poem should feel
like it spoke in your voice.

Acknowledgments

Thanks Sayoni, for asking me to do this book!
Thanks Tina, for patience, support and firefighting on all fronts!
Thanks Matthew, for the title!
Thanks to the A-list – Anshumani, Alakta, Aabir, Aashya – for instant sms-es and wish-lists! And thank you, dear Antara, for your eagle-eyes!

The following poems
'After the Journey'
'Entries'
'Try Describing'
are from my poetry collection *Sight May Strike You Blind* (Sahitya Akademi, 2007, reprint 2008)
as are
'Meditation on a Painted Egg' (original title 'Object Lesson: Eight')
'Poem for my Tortoise' (original title 'Object Lesson: Nine).

The poem
'Girl, Adopted'
first appeared in the online journal *Kritya*.

The poems
'I'm Sick of Learning Lochinvar'
'Word-Balloon'
'Boys Meant Skinny'
'My First Death'
'High-Altitude Sickness'
'Used To Be'
'On Blushes, Jealousy and Skirts'
'The Electric Caterpillar'
first appeared on Infochangeindia.org: Poetry for change.

The poems
'Blue Heron'
'Yogurt and Cinnamon Dessert With Rose Geraniums and Peach'
won an Honourable Mention in the Dorothy Sargent Rosenberg Memorial Fund 2005 Awards.

The poem
'The Mysteries of a Japanese Bento'
first appeared in *Wasafiri* (UK), Issue 49, Summer 2006.

The poems
'Idli-Pom'
'Very Fishy'
'Explained'
'Easy'
'Frankie'
first appeared in *The Tenth Rasa: An Anthology of Indian Nonsense* (Penguin India, 2007).